Sanitary Techniques in Food Service

Sanitary Techniques
in Food Service

Karla Longrée, Ph.D.
Professor of Institution Management, Emeritus
Cornell University, Ithaca, New York

and

Gertrude G. Blaker, Ph.D.
Associate Professor of Food Science and Nutrition
Colorado State University,
Fort Collins, Colorado

John Wiley & Sons, Inc.
New York • London • Sydney • Toronto

Preface

The book is written to serve as:

1. A text for teachers and students of junior colleges, community colleges, technical institutes, trade institutes, special culinary institutes, and similar institutions.
2. A teaching aid for teachers of vocational high schools and special training schools for adults; for instructors developing materials for educating food handlers; for teachers in manpower programs; and the like.

In this country we have an expanding field of employment for middle and first-line management personnel in the food-service industry. We have an increasing and unmet need for assistant dietitians, food-production supervisors, assistant managers, dietary technicians, floor food-service supervisors in hospitals, school-lunch managers, dietary supervisors in nursing homes, and similar technical positions in the food service industry. Technical courses in food-service administration and management are offered in the type of schools listed above. These schools attract a sizable number of young persons who do not plan to attend a four-year course of study in a university.

Sanitation is an important aspect of quantity food preparation and service. To be effective, principles and techniques of food sanitation should be taught in a systematic way as an essential part of early training. Ideally, sanitation should become a way of life for the employee before he assumes his first position in a food-service operation. Faulty notions and faulty techniques, once ingrained, are most difficult to change.

In many work situations, middle- and first-line management personnel function as instructors of the production, service, and sanitation staff. As future supervisors and assistant managers, or even as managers and administrators, students enrolled in vocational courses in food-service administration should at that time build a sound foundation in the principles and techniques of sanitation.

v

Sanitary Techniques in Food Service consists of four parts: (I) "Food Sanitation and Microbiology," (II) "Food Spoilage and Foodborne Illnesses," (III) "Sanitary Practice," and (IV) "Education and Training in Sanitation of Food-Service Personnel." In this volume, accepted facts are stated while controversial literature is not discussed. Directions are given about purchasing a sound food supply, about the sanitary techniques of preparing, holding and serving food, and about the sanitary care of the physical plant, equipment, and utensils. Certain scientific background information is assembled in tables and presented in the appendix for the benefit of teachers and those students who desire to study in greater depth. Study Questions and Suggested Readings follow each part.

The future food handler, it is hoped, will become convinced of the fact that the public health approach to food sanitation is one of preventing hazards from arising, and that he—the food handler—plays a very important role in the business of serving wholesome meals to the public.

KARLA LONGRÉE
GERTRUDE G. BLAKER

Contents

List of Tables   ix

List of Procedures   xi

PART I *Food Sanitation and Microbiology*   1

SECTION

  A The Meaning of Food Sanitation   3
  B Basic Facts about Microorganisms   6
  C Definition of Terms   16
  D Important Facts in Brief for Part I   21

Study Questions for Part I   22

Readings for Part I   22

PART II *Food Spoilage and Foodborne Illnesses*   23

SECTION

  A Food Spoilage   25
  B Transmission of Disease through Food   28
  C Food Poisonings and Food Infections Caused by Bacteria   33
  D Food Poisoning Caused by Agents Other than Microorganisms   48
  E Reporting and Investigating Foodborne Illnesses   50
  F Important Facts in Brief for Part II   54

Study Questions for Part II   56

Readings for Part II   56

PART III *Sanitary Practice*   57

SECTION

  A Clean Facility (Physical Plant)   59
  B Clean Equipment and Utensils   78
  C A Sound Food Supply: Purchasing and Sanitary Storage   120

D The Sanitation-Conscious Food Handler 146

E Sanitary Procedures of Preparing and Holding
Food: General Principles 152

F Techniques for Handling Specific Hazardous Menu Items 170

G Important Facts in Brief for Part III 187

Study Questions for Part III 189

Readings for Part III 189

PART IV *Education and Training in Sanitation of
Food Service Personnel* 191

Readings for Part IV 196

Visual Aids 196

Appendix 197

Index 217

List of Tables

Table   *Page*

1. Important Types of Bacterial Food Poisoning and Food Infection   34
2. Floor Cleaning   71
3. Safety of Milk and Other Dairy Products   122
4. Safety of Eggs   129
5. Safety of Meat   134
6. Safety of Poultry, Fish, and Shellfish   138
7. Safety of Canned Foods and Precooked Frozen Foods   141
8. Safety of Creamed Items   171
9. Safety of Egg-Thickened Desserts: Stirred Custards, Cream Fillings, Puddings, and Cream-Filled Baked Goods   172
10. Safety of Meringued Pies   173
11. Safety of Hollandaise   174
12. Safety of Menu Items Containing Uncooked Egg   175
13. Safety of Soups and Soup Base   176
14. Safety of Fish and Shellfish Items: General Directions   177
15. Safety of Gravies   178
16. Safety of Meat Roasts (Other than Pork and Ham)   179
17. Safety of Cooked Pork and Ham   180
18. Safety of Poultry Items   181
19. Safety of Deboned Poultry   182
20. Safety of Salads (Potato, Meat, Poultry, Egg, and Seafood)   184
21. Safety of Sandwiches Made with Meat, Poultry, Egg, and Fish   185
22. Safety of Hot Menu Items Made with Ground, Minced, Flaked, Cubed, or Otherwise Comminuted Meat, Poultry, Egg, Fish, and Shellfish   186

Appendix

I. Transmission of Microorganisms Causing Human Respiratory Diseases   198

II.   Transmission of Microorganisms Causing Human Intestinal
      Diseases   203
III. Transmission of Microorganisms Causing Diseases in
      Animals and Humans   206
IV.   Botulism   208
V.   Staphylococcus Food Poisoning   210
VI.   Salmonella Food Infection (Salmonellosis)   212
VII. Perfringens Food Poisoning   214

List of Procedures

1. How to Clean Food Slicer   83
2. How to Clean Vegetable Chopper   84
3. How to Clean Vertical Cutter/Mixer   85
4. How to Clean Food Mixer   88
5. How to Clean Steak Machine   88
6. How to Clean Power Meat Saw   89
7. How to Clean Food Grinder   90
8. How to Clean Bench Can Opener   91
9. How to Clean Platform Scales   91
10. How to Clean Table Scales (Even Balance)   92
11. How to Clean Portion-Control Scales   92
12. How to Clean Chopping Boards   92
13. How to Clean Pots, Pans, and Small Utensils (Manual)   93
14. How to Clean Pots, Pans, and Small Utensils (Machine)   94
15. How to Wash Dishes, Glassware, and Flatware (Flite-Type
    Machine)   95
16. How to Clean Rotary Toaster   96
17. How to Clean Automatic Toaster   96
18. How to Clean Coffee Urn   97
19. How to Clean Potato Peeler   98
20. How to Clean Steam-Jacketed Kettle   99
21. How to Clean Stack Steamer   100
22. How to Clean Hi-Pressure Steamer   100
23. How to Clean Electric Overhead Broiler (Salamander)   102
24. How to Clean Gas Frialator   102
25. How to Clean Electric Frialator   104
26. How to Clean Electric Fry Pan   104
27. How to Clean Ranges   106
28. How to Clean Range Ovens   108
29. How to Clean Electric Stack Ovens   109

30. How to Clean Gas Stack Ovens   109
31. How to Clean Pot-and-Pan Machine   110
32. How to Clean Flite-Type Dishwasher   111
33. How to Clean Ice-Cream Cabinet   112
34. How to Clean Reach-in Refrigerator   114
35. How to Clean Steam Table   115
36. How to Clean Dish Trucks   116
37. How to Clean Baker's Table   116
38. How to Clean Kitchen Tables   118
39. How to Clean Metal Shelving (Pot and Pan Storage)   119

Sanitary Techniques in Food Service

PART I

Food Sanitation and Microbiology

SECTION A

The Meaning of Food Sanitation

In the United States, probably several million cases of foodborne illness occur each year. This happens in spite of the fact that the food-processing industry, aided by government health authorities, does a good job in providing us with a wholesome food supply. Something is going wrong somewhere. What are the causes that may change sound food to poison, and where are these undesirable forces at work? The answer is, many of the occurrences of foodborne illness can be traced to the mishandling of food in quantity food-service operations.

A report may read like this "More than two hundred children became ill after eating chicken-salad sandwiches; a number of victims had to be hospitalized. . . . The chicken salad had been prepared from warm ingredients and had been left out in the kitchen for several hours. . . ." Or it may read this way "A gay banquet ended sadly when more then half the guests became ill with violent nausea, vomiting, and diarrhea during the night. . . . Shrimp cocktail was determined to be the offending food. The frozen cooked shrimp had been defrosted overnight in warm water and had remained for an unknown number of hours at temperatures at which rapid bacterial growth was possible. . . . The shrimp were chilled before they were served, but the chilling would not eliminate the bacteria. . . ." As you will have noticed, bacteria caused these foodborne illnesses.

The food-service industry is obligated to change this deplorable situation. It is estimated* that Americans eat 25% of their food outside the home. Several million persons are busy preparing and serving the meals, and the food-service industry is predicted to grow to an even larger volume in the near future.

Preparing and serving wholesome food to the public is a very important obligation of the food-service industry. It is an obligation that can only be

* From West, Wood, and Harger, *Food Service in Institutions* (for complete reference of the book, see the Readings for Part II).

fulfilled if everyone in every establishment understands what sanitation is, appreciates its importance, and practices it in whatever task he performs.

What is the meaning of sanitation in food service? Food sanitation pertains to both the cleanliness and the wholesomeness of food—food that is appealing to the eye and the palate, and that will not make us ill. Practicing sanitation means applying sanitary measures at every stage of the operation—purchasing, receiving, storing, preparing, and serving—for the sake of cleanliness and for the sake of protecting the health of the public served.

Sanitary practice, then, is concerned with the purchase of a sound food supply and its sanitary storage; with the adequacy of the physical plant and its maintenance regarding repairs and cleanliness; with the adequacy and cleanliness of storage facilities, equipment, and utensils; with sanitary dishwashing operations; with the good health, good personal hygiene, and good working habits of the food handler; with the sanitary manipulation of food and effective time-temperature control throughout preparation and service; and finally, with the education of food-service employees in the various aspects of sanitation in a food-service operation.

It has been aptly stated by the National Sanitation Foundation,* (a nonprofit, noncommercial organization that seeks and provides solutions to problems involving cleanliness in food service), that:

"Sanitation is a way of life. It is the quality of living that is expressed in the clean home, the clean farm, the clean business and industry, the clean neighborhood, the clean community. Being a way of life, it must come from within the people; it is nourished by knowledge and grows as an obligation and an ideal in human relations."

For all who are in the food-service business, whether they are managers, supervisors, or workers, sanitation can become a way of life through understanding and knowledge. Everyone needs to become aware of and understand the reasons for the evil and dangerous consequences that lack of sanitation creates, and then go ahead and take the second step, the positive approach of action, the unrelenting practice of sanitation, around the clock, every day of the week, every week of the year.

Food-service operators and food handlers have control over the stomachs of millions of persons. It is largely their responsibility whether the food they serve to the public is wholesome. Therefore, food-service operators and food handlers are part of "public health." It is hoped that in the near future, every person in charge of a food-service operation and every food handler will be a trained person, a professional. Some formal training in

* Ann Arbor, Michigan.

basic principles of food service should be required of everyone who handles food, and sanitation should be an important part of such training. The training should be terminated by an examination which the trainee must successfully pass before he is allowed to operate or manage a food service, or to handle food served to the public.

Basic Facts About Microorganisms

To understand food sanitation, one must understand the activities of microorganisms, which are the cause of most foodborne illnesses. Sanitation is largely concerned with the removal or other effective control of microorganisms in food and everything that touches food.

Microorganisms are microscopically small, living organisms that take up nourishment, give up waste products, and multiply. Some are man's friend, some his enemy, and some neither.

Microorganisms are important in connection with food sanitation, because certain disease-producing kinds may be transmitted through food, and other kinds may multiply in food to high numbers and cause so-called food poisoning. Most microorganisms causing foodborne illnesses are bacteria; but viruses, protozoa, and trichinae are other microorganisms that can cause foodborne illnesses. Even certain molds may render food unwholesome.

Microorganisms, especially bacteria and molds, are easily spread and found almost everywhere. We should know what they look like, how they grow, and how they may be killed. We shall understand foodborne illnesses better if we understand these facts; and we shall understand that we can do a great deal about preventing these incidences by preventing our food from becoming contaminated; by preventing multiplication of contaminants in the food; by killing the contaminants by proper heating of the food; by removing contaminants from tables, chopping boards, and other equipment and utensils through proper cleaning; and by using other sanitary practices described in this book.

BACTERIA

Bacteria and Man

Some kinds work for us, some against us, and some do neither.

Many kinds of bacteria are man's friend; others are neither beneficial

6

nor harmful; still others are undesirable but not harmful; and some are harmful because they spoil man's food or are illness-producing or pathogenic to man.

Beneficial bacteria aid man in the manufacture of food items such as cheese, buttermilk, sauerkraut, and pickles.

Benign bacteria are neither beneficial nor harmful to man. The majority of bacteria belong in this group.

Spoilage bacteria are capable of decomposing our food supply and causing economic loss on all levels—the world, the nation, and the individual wholesaler, retailer, and food-service operator.

Pathogenic bacteria are capable of causing illness. This latter group is very important to us from a public-health point of view, and therefore requires our attention throughout this book.

Size and Shape

Bacteria are single-celled, thin-walled living organisms that take in nourishment, produce waste, and multiply. They may be round cocci or elongated rods, or they may be commalike or corkscrewlike. The round cocci may cling together in various numbers and patterns: diplococci are pairs of cells, staphylococci form grapelike clusters, and streptococci form chains. Some rods, too, may cling together in chains (Figure 1).

Spores

The majority of bacteria possess a fragile and thin wall around the cell; they are called vegetative cells. Some bacteria are able to produce spores that are thick-walled and tough. Spores are able to withstand cold, heat, drought, and other adverse conditions which the thin-walled vegetative cells cannot endure.

Reproduction

When thin-walled bacterial cells multiply, they simply split in two. This process repeats itself many times, as long as conditions are favorable. If

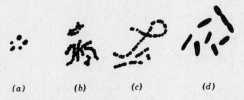

(a)   (b)   (c)   (d)

Figure 1. Some bacterial shapes. (a) Single cocci; (b) staphylococci; (c) streptococci; (d) rods.

(a)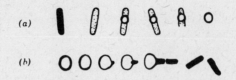

(b)

Figure 2. Bacterial spores. (a) Formation of spore inside vegetable cell; (b) spore, its germination into a vegetative cell and subsequent division into a new crop of vegetative cells. (Adapted from Burdon & Williams, 1964).

nourishment is of the right kind and plentiful, if temperature conditions are favorable, and if there are no growth-inhibiting substances present, reproduction can proceed very rapidly.

On the other hand, spores must germinate before they can multiply. Figure 2 illustrates how a spore forms a new, thin-walled cell from which a new crop of bacteria is now being formed through splitting.

The Growth Curve

When bacterial cells multiply by splitting, they pass through various stages. When scientists study the multiplication of bacteria, they count the number of cells over a certain period of time and plot the results on graph paper. Figure 3 shows a typical growth curve. The time span over which the curve stretches and the highest number of cells produced depend on many factors. Under conditions favorable for growth, a high number of cells is reached in a short time—in fact, in just a few hours. The number of bacteria may double in as little as 15 minutes. Here is an example: if we

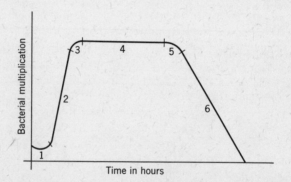

Figure 3. The growth curve of bacteria. Six stages are shown. (1) The lag phase—no multiplication occurs. (2) The phase of rapid multiplication. (3) Multiplication becomes much slower. (4) Growth and death cancel out. (5) Death proceeds faster than growth. (6) Death phase.

had only one single cell and it divided once in 15 minutes, and every young cell divided every 15 minutes thereafter, this first cell would multiply into approximately 1,000,000 (one million) cells in as little as 5 hours. If for some reason the division of cells is slowed down and takes twice as long, or 30 minutes, production of the same one million cells takes as long as 10 hours.

We must keep this important fact before us, because it is applicable to conditions in food service. We must learn under what circumstances of food preparation bacteria are likely to multiply rapidly and what we can do to prevent this.

Toxin Production

While actively multiplying in food, some bacteria are able to form poisonous toxins that they release into the food. Some of these toxins are so powerful that the person eating the poisoned food can become seriously ill and even die. An example of a deadly poison is the dreaded botulinum toxin. Other toxins are violent in their immediate effect, but their victims usually recover. Again, others are quite mild; to become ill, a person would have to eat a great deal of the poisonous food or to be rather sensitive to the toxin.

We shall learn more about toxins in connection with food poisoning (Part II-C).

Conditions for Growth and Toxin Production

In order to multiply, bacteria must have food, moisture, and warmth. Some bacteria must have air and others do better without air; for still others, it does not seem to matter one way or the other.

Food. The various kinds of bacteria have different food needs. However, the bacteria we are concerned with here—the illness-producing ones—prefer the nonacid to acid (sour) foods. Among the nonacid foods liked by bacteria are items high in protein such as milk, eggs, meat, poultry, fish, and shellfish. Most vegetables are slightly acid; therefore, bacteria multiply slowly in them. Fruits, tomatoes, pickles, sauerkraut, and items rendered acidic through the addition of vinegar, lemon juice or other acid ingredients, are least liked by bacteria and are potentially safe foods.

The U. S. Public Health Service* has an excellent term for those foods in which bacteria thrive best—"potentially hazardous foods." This term indicates that it is possible for these foods to become a health hazard. The Public Health Service says:

* U.S. Department of Health, Education and Welfare, Public Health Service (1962) *Food Service Sanitation Manual, Including Model Food Service Sanitation Ordinance and Code.* PHS Publ. 934, Washington, D.C.

"POTENTIALLY HAZARDOUS FOODS shall mean any perishable food which consists in whole or in part of milk or milk products, eggs, meat, poultry, fish, shellfish, or other ingredients capable of supporting rapid and progressive growth of infectious or toxigenic microorganisms."

However, these foods do not *have* to become a hazard if precautions are taken so that they are not mishandled in their processing, preparation and service.

Moisture. Bacteria require moisture for growth. Dry foods such as sugar, flour, dry cereal, dry rice, cookies, biscuits, and other dry baked products are not good media for bacterial multiplication. Unfortunatley, a great number of the prepared menu items that we serve contain sufficient moisture for bacterial growth.

Warmth. The majority of bacteria thrive best at warm temperatures, from 60 to 120°F. Disease-producing organisms, or pathogens, grow best near body temperature. Multiplication is slowed down as the temperature is raised or lowered, and ceases at temperatures near 140° or higher, and at temperatures near 45° and lower.

Some bacteria thrive best at high temperatures, 113°F or higher. These are the heat-loving, or thermophilic bacteria. Among these are the bacteria causing spoilage in canned foods when these are kept in hot storage rooms. Other bacteria are able to grow well in a cool environment—in fact, at refrigerator temperatures or below. They are the cold-loving, or psychrophilic bacteria. They are frequently responsible for spoiling food stored too long in the refrigerator.

Bacteria do not multiply in solidly frozen foods, but freezing does not kill all bacteria, either. About one half of the bacteria survive the freezing of foods and the average periods of freezer storage. The survivors may again multiply when the food has been defrosted and has warmed up to 45°F and above.

For all practical purposes, bacterial growth is possible within the temperature range of 45° and 140°F. From a public-health point of view, this temperature range is called the DANGER ZONE.

Death of Bacteria

Bacteria share with other living beings the fate that sometime they must die. Bacteria die of old age, or because microbial waste products poison them, or because other microorganisms that are their rivals for nourishment cause them to starve. Bacteria may be killed before they die a natural death.

1. Death by Heat. Bacteria vary in their resistance to heat, some kinds being killed more easily than others. Spores are most difficult to kill. Food processors use heat in canning, pasteurizing, curing, and smoking of food. In *canning*, the food is subjected to a harsh heat treatment; the heating must be sufficient to kill the spores of the deadly food-poisoning organism, *Clostridium botulinum*. This organism grows best without air in a sealed can or jar. In *pasteurizing*, milder heating is applied. A good example of a pasteurized product is milk. Pasteurization procedures are carefully worked out to kill the majority of contaminating microorganisms and all the pathogens without destroying important quality characteristics of the food. However, pasteurized products do not possess sterility. Another example of a pasteurized product is egg; the contents of shell eggs must be pasteurized before they are frozen or dried.

Ham is heat treated during the process of *tenderization*, which destroys many, but not all, contaminants. This is an important fact to remember when storing tenderized hams (Part III-C).

Foods may or may not be rendered free from contaminants in the *cooking* process; the type of organism, the nature of the food, and the cooking procedure used, all have an effect. A detailed discussion of this subject will be found in Part III-E and F.

Killing heat is also used—in the form of hot water—to *sanitize* eating

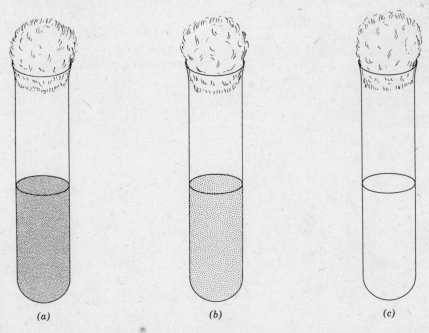

(a)   (b)   (c)

Figure 4. Effect of temperature on bacteria. (a) Growth is good or excellent between 45 and 140°F; (b) growth is very slow below 45°F; (c) boiling kills bacteria.

and food-preparation utensils. The procedures used are discussed in Part III-B.

Figure 4 illustrates the effect of temperature on bacteria.

2. Death by Chemical Agents. Chemicals can and sometimes are used as sanitizing agents in dishwashing and in treating work surfaces such as boards, table tops, and counters.

MOLDS

Molds are a frequent cause of food spoilage. A few molds are suspected of causing illness in man; the problem is currently under investigation. Certain molds used by the dairy industry in processing Blue cheese, Roquefort and Gorgonzola, are considered safe to eat.

Most molds are thread-like, the threads bearing spores. (Figure 5). Molds can be seen as a fuzzy, cottony growth of a variety of colors, on a great variety of foods. Molds can grow on practically all foods—the sweet, the sour, the bitter, the moist, and the dry. They are not choosy regarding temperatures at which they grow. Everyone is familiar with the appearance of mold on refrigerated food, around refrigerator doors, and on damp cellar walls; and of luxurious mold growth on shoes, books, and the like when the weather is hot and humid.

Mold spores are carried about in the air. One little piece of moldy bread can contaminate other foods stored far away. Heating to the boiling point kills molds, including the spores.

Unless a mold is used in the processing of a food, like some cheeses, there is no excuse for a food to be moldy. The presence of moldy, spoiled food indicates poor food management.

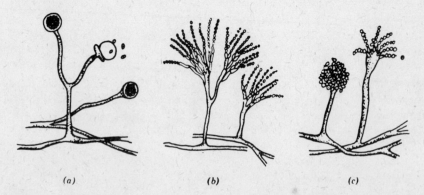

(a)   (b)   (c)

Figure 5. Molds. (a) Mucor; (b) Penicillium; (c) Aspergillus. (Adapted from Burdon & Williams, 1964).

(a) *(b)*

Figure 6. Yeasts and protozoa. (a) Yeasts; (b) protozoa (shown is *Endameba histolytica,* cause of amebic dysentery). (Adapted from Burdon & Williams, 1964).

YEASTS

Yeasts possess microscopically small, thin-walled cells that mutiply by sprouting (Figure 6a). They like sweet liquid foods and are well known for spoiling cider and fruit juices by fermenting them. Yeasts are purposely used in making bread, wine and beer. From a public-health point of view, they are harmless. They can be readily killed by boiling.

VIRUSES

Viruses can also be transmitted through food. Viruses are smaller than the smallest bacteria. They cannot multiply in foods; in fact, they multiply only in living cells of their hosts. Examples of viruses known to have been transmitted through food are those causing infectious hepatitis and polio.

How does a virus such as the hepatitis virus find its way into food? First, from a person who has hepatitis or has recently recovered from this illness. Persons recovering from hepatitis are apt to be carriers for a while (a carrier is a person who appears to be healthy, but who still harbors in him the germs of the disease with which he was ill). When a hepatitis carrier visits the toilet, does not wash his hands thoroughly and then handles food, he contaminates the food with the virus clinging to his hands.

Another source of viruses is sewage-polluted waters (such as streams, lakes, and oceans) and the fish and shellfish harvested from them. A third source may be raw sewage that is allowed to drip onto food or kitchen tables from leaky overhead pipes, or through otherwise faulty plumbing.

PROTOZOA

Protozoa are very small animal-like microorganisms (Figure 6b) that are widely distributed in lakes, ponds, streams, oceans, and in moist soil rich in organic matter. Protozoa may occur in the intestinal tract of man. Several

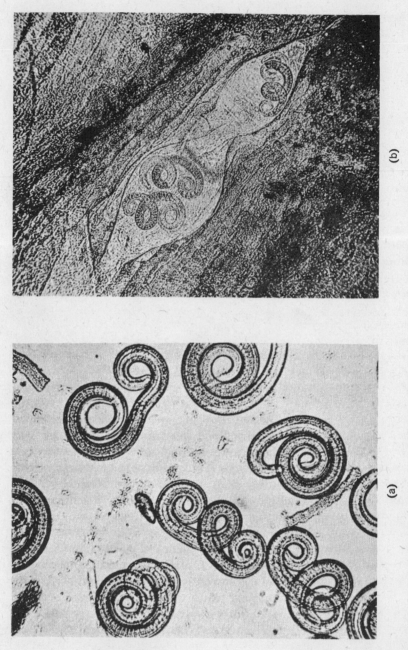

Figure 7. Trichinae. (a) Free; (b) imbedded in muscle meat. (Reprinted by permission of L. B. Jensen.)

of these organisms cause intestinal disorders, the so-called amebic dysenteries. The amebae may be transferred to food with fecal matter clinging to the hands of food handlers who have dysentery or have had the disease and have become carriers of the organism. This shows the necessity of thorough hand washing after a visit to the toilet.

Vegetables and fruits that have had contact with contaminated soil may become contaminated. Fortunately, in the U.S.A. dysentery-producing amebae are not common contaminants of soils on which truck crops are raised.

TRICHINAE

Trichinae are microscopically small, wormlike parasites that cause a disease in hogs, rabbits and bears. The trichinae settle in the muscle meat of the hosts (Figure 7). When we eat undercooked, infested meat, we may also become ill with trichinosis.

Hogs contract the disease by eating uncooked, infested garbage. Fortunately, trichinosis of hogs becomes less prevalent every year. However, one must not take chances. It is important to use proper cooking methods for all pork, rabbit, and bear meat, and to heat these meats to the grey state. Thorough heating kills the trichinae and renders the meat safe for human consumption.

Cutting and grinding of infested raw meat may contaminate cutting boards and grinders; therefore, these surfaces should be thoroughly washed after each use.

SECTION C

Definition of Terms

★*Bacteria* are plantlike single cells that are only visible with the aid of a microscope; they multiply by splitting in two.

Bactericidal is a term that describes a substance capable of killing bacteria.

Bacteriostatic is a term that describes a substance that inhibits the multiplication of bacteria.

★*Botulism* is a frequently fatal type of food poisoning caused by a toxin produced by a spore-forming bacterium under exclusion of air; the bacterium is *Clostridium botulinum*.

Carrier is a person who harbors organisms causing a communicable disease without showing outward signs of illness.

Chilling is cooling above the freezing point. Food is usually chilled by refrigeration.

★*Coccus* (cocci, plural) is a round bacterium.

Coliform bacteria are undesirable in foods. Their presence in some foods, especially seafood, milk, and water, indicates the possibility of contamination with excrement (manure, sewage). One of the species of the group, *Escherichia coli*, is a common inhabitant of the intestinal tract of men and animals.

Communicable diseases are contagious or "catching" diseases. The causative agents are readily transferred from person to person.

★*Clean* means free from dirt, soil, and disease-producing microorganisms.

Contaminated food means food that contains undesirable microorganisms; contamination is the act of contaminating.

Cross contamination means the contamination of clean, wholesome food with illness-producing bacteria adhering to raw food, soiled hands, soiled work surfaces, soiled equipment, soiled utensils, soiled clothing, and the like.

★*Danger zone of bacterial growth* is the temperature range from 45 to 140°F. Within this range, growth of food poisoning bacteria is possible. Food temperatures should not be within this range for longer than 4 hours, and should not be within the 60 to 120°F range for longer than 2 hours.

16

Disinfectant is a chemical agent used to inhibit the growth of, or to destroy, harmful microorganisms.

Epidemic is a disease that affects a large number of persons at the same time; the disease is spread from person to person.

Food handler is a person who handles food in the food-service establishment regardless of whether he actually prepares or serves food.

Food infection is an illness caused by eating food that contains bacteria capable of causing a gastrointestinal infection in the victim.

Food intoxication is a foodborne illness caused by a toxin, or toxins. The toxin, or toxins, may be of bacterial origin.

Food poisoning—see "*Food intoxication.*" The term is frequently widened to include food infections.

Food spoilage is the deterioration of food, making it unfit for human consumption.

Foodborne illness is an illness caused by food that is poisonous or contains pathogenic microorganisms or parasites.

Fungus, Fungi (plural) are threadlike plant microorganisms.

Gastroenteritis is an inflammation of the stomach and the intestinal tract.

Gastrointestinal pertains to the stomach and the intestinal tract.

Generation time is the time that elapses between one division of a bacterial cell into two daughter cells and the next division of each of these daughter cells.

Germicide is an agent used for killing microorganisms.

Growth curve is a curve that depicts the multiplication of bacteria over a period of time.

Growth of bacteria denotes the multiplication of bacteria rather than their increase in size.

Hygiene, personal, refers to the cleanliness of one's body.

Immunization is the process of rendering an individual immune, or restistant, to a disease.

Incubation time refers to the period between infection and the appearance of signs of the disease.

Infections, foodborne, are illnesses caused by swallowing certain pathogenic bacteria present in the food. Food infections may be caused by relatively few cells of highly infectious pathogens that are transmitted by food; or by pathogens that must multiply in the food to high numbers before they make the victim ill.

Infectious refers to the ability of a microorganism to produce an infection in a susceptible host.

Inhibitors of microorganisms are substances that interfere with their growth.

Intoxications, foodborne, are illnesses caused by a toxin, or poison in the food consumed; the toxin may be of bacterial origin.

Lag phase of bacterial growth is the inactive period preceding bacterial multiplication; the cells are there, but they are not yet dividing.

Log phase of bacterial growth is the period of constant and rapid multiplication; the generation times are shortest during this period.

Microorganisms are microscopic plants or animals.

Milliliter is a very small fluid measure; it equals 1/1000 of a liter (or approximately 1/1000 of a quart). The milliliter is used to express bacterial counts in fluids such as water and milk.

Molds are microscopically small plants (fungi) that may appear as fuzzy patches on food. Certain molds produce toxins suspected of causing illness in man.

Multiplication of bacteria, or bacterial growth, takes place by the splitting of a bacterial cell into two, which in turn split into two, and so on.

Optimum means best.

Parasites are organisms that live in living hosts, from which they draw their nutrients. Animals and plants can be parasitic. The latter are not important in connection with foodborne illnesses.

Pasteurization is a process of killing microorganisms in a food (for example, milk) by heating it at well-controlled temperatures (which are considerably below boiling) for specified lengths of time.

Pathogen is an organism causing disease.

Pathogenic means causing disease.

Perishable food is a food that spoils readily. Many of our daily foods are perishable.

pH expresses the acidity or alkalinity of a substance. A pH of 7 indicates that the substance is neither acid nor alkaline. As the pH values increase to 14, the alkalinity increases; as the pH values decrease to 0, the acidity increases. Examples of approximate pH values are lemons, 2.2; apricots, 3.3; tomatoes, 4.4; spinach, 5.5; egg yolk, 6.4; meat, 7.0; and egg white, 8.0.

Pollute means to render foul, unclean, dirty, or contaminated with fecal matter.

Potentially hazardous foods are foods that consist entirely, or in part, of milk, eggs, meat, poultry, fish, or shellfish; or that are for other reasons capable of supporting the growth of microorganisms causing foodborne illness. Many much-handled, lightly heated, or unheated foods are potentially hazardous.

Protozoa are small animal-like microorganisms; some are transmitted through food.

Psychrophilic bacteria are cold-loving bacteria.

Ptomaine food poisoning is a meaningless term that should not be used to denote food poisoning.

Putrefaction is the process of becoming putrid or rotten.

Putrid means rotten or foul-smelling.

Recontaminating means contaminating anew food or surfaces previously rendered free from bacteria.

Respiratory tract is the part of the anatomy that serves the function of breathing or respiration.

Route of disease transmission—see "vehicle of transmission."

Safe temperatures for food are temperatures at which microbial growth is very slow or nil: 45°F and below; and 140°F and above.

Sanitation of food pertains to the wholesomeness and cleanliness of food.

Sanitizing means reducing the number of microorganisms on articles or in substances to levels judged safe by the health authorities. In food service, sanitizing refers to treatments to eliminate pathogenic bacteria from equipment and utensils that are used in the preparation and service of food.

Species refers to one kind of microorganism; a species is a subdivision of a genus. Therefore, a genus is a group of closely related species.

Spoilage of food refers to the deterioration of food, which makes it unfit for human consumption. However, people vary in what they regard as deteriorated or unfit to eat.

Spores are thick-walled bodies formed by some microorganisms, such as molds and certain bacteria. Spores are resistant to heat, drought, and other unfavorable conditions. The soil abounds with spores.

Staph is an abbreviation of staphylococci.

Staphylococci are cocci bunched in grapelike clusters.

Sterile means free of living organisms.

Streptococci are cocci arranged in chains.

Thermoduric bacteria are bacteria capable of surviving exposure to heating processes such as pasteurization and canning.

Thermophilic bacteria are heat-loving bacteria.

Time-temperature control of bacteria in food refers to regulating the length of time for which a food is allowed to remain at certain unsafe temperatures. At unsafe temperatures, bacteria may multiply rather rapidly. At safe temperatures, growth is halted.

Toxic foods are foods that contain toxins; these toxins may or may not stem from microbial growth.

Toxins are poisonous compounds.

Trichinae are small wormlike parasites embedded in pork, rabbit, and bear meat and originating from animals suffering from trichinosis.

Trichinosis in humans is a type of foodborne illness following the eating of trichinae-infested, undercooked pork, rabbit, or bear meat.

Vegetative bacterial cells are thin-walled cells that multiply by splitting.

Vehicle of transmission refers to the route by which a pathogen is passed on from its original source to a victim. Vehicles of transmission can be soiled hands, sewage, water, air, soil, food, rats, mice, flies, cockroaches, and soiled food-preparation equipment and utensils.

Viruses are very small pathogens that multiply in the living cells of their hosts; they do not multiply in cooked food.

Wholesome food is sound food, fit for human consumption.

Yeasts are microorganisms that multiply by budding and may cause spoilage of fruit juices by fermenting sugar to alcohol and carbon dioxide. Yeasts are used in preparing yeast-leavened doughs, wine, and beer.

Important Facts in Brief for Part 1

- Bacteria are very small and are everywhere.
- Certain kinds of bacteria are harmful to man, some causing food spoilage, and others causing disease.
- Bacteria causing communicable (or catching) diseases can be transmitted through food.
- Certain so-called food-poisoning bacteria may cause illness if allowed to multiply in food to high numbers, after which the food is served and eaten.
- Bacterial spores are very hardy and survive harsh heat treatments and other adverse conditions.
- Vegetative bacterial cells reproduce by splitting in two; this process is very rapid when conditions are favorable.
- Bacteria need food, moisture, and warmth for growth. With respect to the safety of foods, the temperature range in which growth is possible is called the DANGER ZONE. This zone ranges from 45 to 140°F. Growth is excellent between 60 and 120°F.
- Bacteria can be killed by heat; to kill spores requires more heat than to kill the delicate, vegetative cells.
- Heat is used to kill pathogenic bacteria in canning and pasteurizing.
- Cooking temperatures do not always suffice to kill pathogenic bacteria.

Study Question for Part 1

1. In your own words, explain what is meant by sanitation as it pertains to food service.
2. Define the term microorganisms; give examples of microorganisms of importance in connection with food sanitation.
3. Describe the growth curve of bacterial mutiplication.
4. Define pasteurization.
5. Can viruses multiply in cooked foods? Explain.
6. What are protozoa? Can protozoa be transmitted through food?
7. Define trichinosis.
8. Explain psychrophilic, thermophilic, and thermoduric.
9. Can bacteria be killed by heat? Explain.
10. Are bacteria killed when food is frozen? Explain.
11. What are important differences between vegetative bacterial cells and bacterial spores? Explain.

Readings for Part 1

Burdon, K. L., and R. P. Williams. *Microbiology*. 5th ed. Macmillan Co., New York. 1964.

Frazier, William C. *Food Microbiology*. 2nd ed. McGraw-Hill Book Co., New York. 1967.

Frobisher, Martin. *Fundamentals of Microbiology*. 7th ed. W. B. Saunders Co., Philadelphia, London. 1962.

Hobbs, Betty. *Food Poisoning and Food Hygiene*. 2nd ed. Edward Arnold Ltd., London. 1968. Part I-2.

Longrée, Karla. *Quantity Food Sanitation*. 2nd ed. Wiley-Interscience, a division of John Wiley and Sons, Inc. New York. 1972. Chapter II.

PART II

Food Spoilage and Foodborne Illnesses

SECTION A

Food Spoilage

What is food spoilage? Spoilage refers to food decomposition as well as to other forms of damage. Food spoilage can cause considerable financial loss to the food-service business, but does not necessarily represent a health hazard. Much spoiled food is not eaten and is simply thrown out. Spoilage may be recognized by the food's appearance, smell, taste, consistency, or a combination of these. However, foods that harbor food-poisoning bacteria or other pathogens usually *appear* to be sound and good to eat, although they are actually dangerous to health.

Most foods will eventually spoil, the so-called perishables spoiling most readily. For the sake of convenience, we may classify foods on the basis of their perishability or stability as follows:

1. *Nonperishable or stable foods.* These foods do not spoil unless they are handled without care. Examples are sugar, macaroni, dry beans, flour, spaghetti, noodles, and other staples.

2. *Somewhat (semi) perishable foods.* These foods will remain free from spoilage for a long time. Examples are nuts, potatoes, and waxed vegetables (for example, rutabagas); frozen foods, provided these are kept solidly frozen at 0°F; and canned foods, if stored no longer than a year and in cool, dry storage rooms.

Frozen foods must be expected to contain bacteria, since freezing does not kill all bacteria, by any means. When frozen foods are defrosted, they are again highly perishable. Bacteria injurious to health may begin to multiply when the DANGER ZONE (which begins at 45°F) has been entered.

Canned foods have excellent keeping quality because the contents of the sealed can are practically free from bacteria, the dangerous bacteria having been removed in the canning process. Some heat-loving and hard-to-kill thermoduric spores of certain bacteria may remain, however. As we learned earlier, heat-loving bacteria are able to grow at warm temperatures. We also learned that certain bacteria grow without air. Therefore, if spores of

25

heat-loving, air-hating bacteria are present in canned food and the can is stored at very warm temperatures, such as 113°F and higher, these spores may resume growth and the contents of the can may spoil. Other types of spoilage of canned goods are also possible; for example, when a can has a leak, bacteria may penetrate into the can and spoil the food. Contents of purposely opened cans may also spoil if stored improperly or for too long.

Signs of spoilage of canned foods are:

(a) Cans that are leaky, corroded, or rusty.

(b) Cans that are bulgy.

(c) Contents that spurt out when opening can.

(d) Contents that appear bubbly, slimy, decomposed, or moldy.

(e) Contents that smell putrid or sulphurous.

(*Note.* Contents may be poisonous. Do not taste from a can of doubtful wholesomeness. Discard it [see also pages 36 to 37, Botulism, and Tables 10 and IV].)

3. *Perishable foods.* This group is a large one and contains most of our daily foods, such as milk and other dairy foods, meat, poultry, eggs, fish, shellfish, fruits, and vegetables. All prepared menu items are perishable; so are canned foods once the can has been opened; and frozen items once they have thawed.

What are the signs of spoilage? The signs of spoilage of perishables vary with the different types of food, the cause of spoilage, and the environment. Spoilage can be caused by overmaturity, the activity of microorganisms, frost, heat-drying, excessive humidity, or combinations of various causes. The visible signs can be softening, hardening, leaking, discoloration, shriveling, moldiness, or bubbling. There can be off-odors such as moldy, yeasty, putrid, musty and sulphuric off-odors. And there can be off-flavors such as rancid, sour, alcoholic, bitter, yeasty, and putrid ones.

Spoilage must be prevented by appropriate storage. Purchase and proper storage of foods is discussed in Part III-C.

Cooked foods may show the various signs of spoilage listed above; or they may not show any signs and yet have become dangerous, sometimes within hours, due to the activity of microorganisms capable of causing food intoxication (poisoning) or gastrointestinal infections. This treacherous fact must be remembered by all who prepare and serve food. Since there frequently are no noticeable signs of spoilage, one cannot rely on signs to judge cooked items for wholesomeness. One must plan, prepare, hold, and serve food in a way that assures its wholesomeness. One must exercise certain definite precautions in the care of leftovers.

Foodborne Illnesses

In the following presentation foodborne illnesses are divided into three groups. It is important that the basis for this grouping is understood before the reader proceeds.

1. Illnesses Caused Through Transmission of Disease Germs

The food may transmit pathogenic germs from one person to another, much as germs are passed from person to person through other soiled objects such as money, doorknobs, railings, common drinking cups, and the like. Food serves as a mere vehicle of disease transmission. Transmission of human and animal pathogens to humans by way of food is possible.

2. Food Poisonings and Food Infections Caused by Bacteria

The terms food poisoning and food infections refer to a violent illness of the stomach and intestinal tract (known as gastroenteritis) following the consumption of the offending food.

The offending food contains, in general, high numbers of bacteria that are capable of producing the gastroenteritis suffered by the victim. Some of these pathogens are able to release toxins into the food; these toxins are the direct cause of the illness (an intoxication). Other pathogens do not act until swallowed, whereupon they cause an infection of the gastrointestinal tract.

3. Food Poisoning Caused by Agents Other than Microorganisms

The offending food contains poisonous chemicals, or the food is a poisonous plant or animal.

Transmission of Disease Through Food

I. TRANSMISSION OF GERMS OF HUMAN ORIGIN

What are these diseases?

Most of the diseases transmitted by food are known to be those of the human respiratory and the intestinal tract. Important transmissible diseases are the common cold, septic sore throat, sinus infection, scarlet fever, tonsil and adenoid infections, pneumonia, trench mouth, diphtheria, tuberculosis, influenza, typhoid and paratyphoid fevers, the dysenteries, cholera, and infectious hepatitis. The organisms causing the diseases are bacteria, protozoa, or viruses. See Tables I and II, Appendix.

How are they transmitted from man to food? (Fig. 8 and 9).

Ill Food Handler

Respiratory illnesses are commonly transmitted through discharges from mouth and nose while coughing and sneezing. Hands and handkerchiefs soiled with discharges from the mouth and nose are also sources; so are tasting spoons used more than once without cleaning. Displayed food can be contaminated by the coughs and sneezes of customers as well as those of personnel.

Disorders of the intestinal tract and infectious hepatitis may be transmitted to food and thereafter to other persons, if the food handler does not wash, or does not thoroughly wash, his hands after visiting the toilet.

Principles of Control. Persons acutely ill with respiratory, intestinal, or other contagious disorders, must not handle food. Carriers of pathogens must not handle food. Displayed food must be protected—as much as is feasible—from the coughs, sneezes, and hands of customers. Food handlers must thoroughly wash the hands after visiting the toilet and after their hands have become soiled in some other way. (see Part III-D).

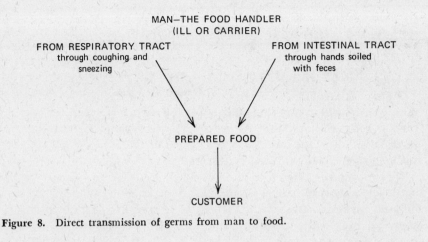

Figure 8.   Direct transmission of germs from man to food.

What other vehicles of transmission are there?

Besides the immediate transmission of pathogens from the food handler or customer to prepared food and from there to the next person or persons, additional routes of transmission are possible. Figure 9 illustrates various ones. They are sewage, and sewage-polluted water, soil and food; rodents

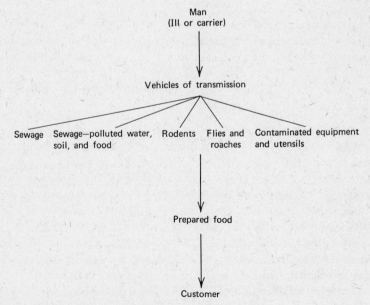

Figure 9.   Transmission of germs to food by various routes.

(rats and mice); insects (flies and cockroaches); and pathogen-contaminated work surfaces, cooking equipment and utensils, china, flatware, and glasses.

Sewage and Sewage-Polluted Water, Soil, and Food

Sewage consists largely of man's wastes. Therefore, raw, untreated sewage must be expected to contain pathogens that have been eliminated from the human body. Examples are the germs causing typhoid and paratyphoid fevers, dysentery, and infectious hepatitis. On the food-service premises, sewage may contaminate food and equipment through faulty plumbing.

If raw sewage is allowed to drain or flow into drinking water, wells, rivers, lakes, and ocean bays, it is not only contaminating the water itself but also the fish and shellfish living therein. Therefore, privies and septic tanks should be sufficiently removed from wells. Raw sewage should be treated before it is directed into rivers, lakes and oceans. Shellfish to be used as food should be harvested from unpolluted waters only.

If raw sewage is used to fertilize fields, the soil becomes contaminated and so do the crops grown on such soil. This is why raw sewage should not be used in the raising of vegetables and fruit.

Principles of Control. Purchase food (in particular, shellfish) from sources approved by the health authorities (see Part III-C).

Rodents and Insects

Rats and mice are rodents that can transmit disease if they are permitted access to the food-service department. Rats in particular are notorious for transmitting disease. The presence of rodent excreta is a sure sign of the presence of these dangerous animals. Rats and mice carry disease-producing germs on their feet, in their fur, and in their intestinal tract. Rats love to roam and feed in garbage dumps and sewers.

Principles of Control. Rats and mice must not be tolerated in a food-service establishment. They must be eradicated and their reentry must be prevented (see Part III-A).

The housefly is the type of fly commonly associated with man's living quarters and eating places, but also with toilets, barns, manure, garbage, and other filth. This crisscrossing from filth to food makes the fly a menace in the food service establishment.

As the fly feeds on a food, it periodically regurgitates liquid from its crop to dissolve the food for easier uptake. This regurgitated liquid may contain disease-producing germs. The fly also carries germs on its feet.

Cockroaches are common pests in kitchens and bakeshops. Like the flies, they contaminate food with their mouth parts, feet, and droppings. They, too, regurgitate filth onto clean food while they feed on it.

Principles of Control. Flies and cockroaches must be eradicated and kept out of the areas where food is prepared and served. Also, they must not be permitted access to toilets and garbage (see Part III-A).

Contaminated Equipment and Utensils

Disease-producing organisms can be transmitted through equipment and utensils if these have been touched by ill, or carrier-type, food handlers and customers; or visited by flies and cockroaches; or exposed to dripping sewage or to sewage that has backed up into sinks or other drainage pipes due to faulty plumbing; or through contact with contaminated water and food.

Principles of Control. Equipment and utensils must be protected from becoming contaminated through contact with the above sources of contamination. They must be maintained in a sanitary condition at all times (see Part III-B).

II. TRANSMISSION OF GERMS OF ANIMAL ORIGIN

What are these diseases?

Only diseases of present importance will be discussed. Great strides have been made to eradicate some diseases that in the past greatly threatened animals as well as humans, such as brucellosis. This is a disease of cattle that can be transmitted to humans through unpasteurized or improperly pasteurized milk.

A disease of wild rabbits, tularemia, is of greater importance to the homemaker than to managers of quantity food-service operations. In the U.S.A., wild rabbit is not apt to be served in commercial food service.

Still important is trichinosis, a disease of hogs that is transmissable to humans if meat containing trichinae is consumed. This may happen when pork is undercooked. This same organism also causes trichinosis in bears and rabbits. Thorough cooking destroys the trichinae. For more detailed information on trichinosis see Table III, Appendix.

In summary, the principles of control of disease transmission through food are:

1. Persons ill with, or carriers of, contagious diseases must not handle food.
2. All food handlers must observe the rules of personal hygiene. They

must thoroughly wash their hands after a sneeze or cough and after visiting the toilet.

3. The food supply should come from uncontaminated sources.

4. Rodents and insects must be strictly controlled in the food-service establishment.

5. Equipment and utensils used in food preparation and service must be maintained in a sanitary condition at all times.

SECTION C

Food Poisonings and Food Infections
Caused by Bacteria

Food poisonings and bacterial infections are usually called simply "food poisoning." These illnesses are characterized by a violent form of upset of the stomach and intestines (gastroenteritis), which follows the consumption of the food in which the offending bacteria were given a chance to multiply. *Bacterial food poisoning is the result of the mishandling of food.*

The time between the consumption of the food and the appearance of the symptoms (called the incubation time) may vary. The violence of the symptoms, such as nausea, vomiting, and cramps of the stomach and intestines (gastrointestinal tract), may vary also. Variation in incubation time and intensity of discomfort depend on:

1. The type of organism causing the illness; some cause a more severe illness than others.
2. The susceptibility of the person; the very young, the aged, the sick, and the feeble are more susceptible.
3. The number of bacteria or the amount of toxin consumed; the greater the number of bacteria and the greater the amount of toxin swallowed, the quicker and more severe is the attack.

What is the difference between bacterial food poisoning and bacterial food infection?

True bacterial food poisoning is caused by a poison, or toxin, which the offending bacteria release into the food, thus rendering it poisonous. True food poisoning is also called a food intoxication. Bacterial food infection, however, is not caused by a toxin in the food. Rather, the bacteria set up an infection in the gastrointestinal tract of the victim after having been swallowed by the victim. *In either case, a great number of bacteria must be present in the food before it will make a person sick.*

The presence of large numbers of bacteria in food indicates that some-

33

Table 1. Important Types of Bacterial Food Poisoning and Food Infection

Illness	Cause	Symptoms	Foods Frequently Involved	Principles of Control
BOTULISM (Rare)	Deadly toxin of a spore-forming bacterium, *Clostridium botulinum*, whose source is soil. Toxin is produced under conditions that exclude air. Toxin can be destroyed by boiling food for 15 minutes.	Symptoms appear 12-36 hours after eating poisonous food. They are nausea, vomiting, dizziness, double vision, and difficulty in breathing. Death results in the majority of cases.	Usually underprocessed, home-canned, nonacid food; underprocessed smoked fish.	Do not serve home-canned foods to the public. Keep smoked fish strictly refrigerated at temperatures below 38°F, preferably in the freezer. DO NOT ever taste suspect food; boil for 15 minutes and DISCARD.
STAPH FOOD POISONING (Common)	Toxin of *Staphylococcus aureus*, a bacterium of human origin; its main sources are the nose and throat, and infected lesions. Toxin is not destroyed by ordinary cooking methods.	Symptoms appear 2-3 (up to 6) hours after eating poisonous food. They are nausea, vomiting, diarrhea, and abdominal cramps.	Protein foods, especially items that are handled a great deal and by careless employees who have unsanitary working habits. Staph-contaminated foods that are exposed for several hours to warm temperatures.	Food handlers must be free from infected sores and respiratory illnesses; must practice sanitary working habits, including frequent washing of hands. Keep cold food cold, hot food hot; cool food rapidly to safe temperatures.

Illness	Cause	Symptoms	Foods Frequently Involved	Principles of Control
PERFRINGENS FOOD POISONING (Common)	Large numbers of a spore-forming bacterium, *Clostridium perfringens*; its source is the intestinal tract of humans and animals; soil; and kitchen dust. Meat may be contaminated with it when purchased.	Symptoms appear 8-15 hours after eating poisonous food; they are similar to symptoms caused by "staph," but milder.	Meat and gravy, especially when prepared in advance and held warm for several hours. Since the bacterium is very common, cooked foods are readily recontaminated through contact with soiled cutting boards and other equipment.	Serve meat and gravy soon after cooking. If items must be cooked in advance, chill quickly and keep refrigerated at safe temperatures. Keep equipment in sanitary condition.
SALMONELLA FOOD INFECTION (Common)	Large numbers of *Salmonella* bacteria; their source is the intestinal tract of humans and animals. Meat, poultry, dirty and cracked shell eggs, and products made from these foods may already be contaminated with salmonellae when they reach the kitchen. Seafood from sewage-polluted waters are contaminated.	Symptoms appear 12-24 hours after eating *Salmonella*-contaminated food. They are similar to symptoms caused by "staph." Fever may occur.	Improperly handled and improperly cooked protein foods, especially those that are apt to be contaminated when they reach the kitchen. All items that have contact with fecal matter of human or animal origin (unwashed human hands, feces from rodents and insects). *Salmonella*-contaminated foods that are exposed for several hours to warm temperature.	Purchase meat, poultry, eggs, and shellfish that have been inspected or certified for wholesomeness. Control rodents and insects. Wash hands after visiting toilet and after handling raw meat and poultry. Keep equipment in sanitary cond Keep cold fo hot food hot; rapidly to saf peratures.

thing has gone wrong in the preparation of the offending food—namely, that it has been mishandled.

We shall now discuss important kinds of food poisoning and food infection and methods of control.

BOTULISM—A FOOD INTOXICATION

Botulism is caused by one of the most powerful poisons, the toxin of a bacterium, *Clostridium botulinum* (Table 1). The toxin attacks the nervous system and the victim usually dies because he cannot breathe properly. Botulism is now rare. The illness is more fully described in Table IV, Appendix.

The bacterium causing the poisoning is able to form hardy spores. Certain types (A and B) are found in soil all over the world; one type (E) usually occurs in the bottom of streams, lakes, and oceans. When we swallow the spores (which we frequently do, since they are everywhere) no ill effects follow; the spores do not find man's intestinal tract fit for growth. However, in a sealed can or jar, the bacterium grows well, if the food is not too acid. Therefore, proper processing at adequately high temperatures is required to make processed foods safe. Commercially processed canned or smoked foods are carefully heat-treated to assure that the botulinum spores are killed, yet, cases of botulism from such sources are on record.

Danger signs in cans are bulging; broken seals; rusting; leakage; contents bubbly, spurting out on opening the can; off-color; and off-odor. These danger signs may range from very noticeable to quite obscure.

Warning: Do not try to find out about flavor, because you might become poisoned in the process. The poison *can* be rendered harmless by boiling the food for 15 minutes. Do not even feed suspect food to animals without having rendered it safe by boiling.

Caution: a canned food product containing the toxin will have a tendency to start bubbling as soon as heat is applied. This is due to the fact that tiny bubbles of gas produced by the bacteria expand in heating and finally escape. This bubbling should not be confused with a true boil.

Principles of Control

1. Use only commercially canned food in quantity food service.
2. Refuse donations of home-canned food; they may not have been processed according to the rules for safety from botulism.
3. Purchase canned food from a reliable vendor and store cans in a cool, dry place; use them within a year.

Danger signs in smoked fish

There may be signs of spoilage, such as off-color, off-odor, or change in texture, which would make one suspicious; however, there may not be any such signs.

Spores of the type (E), which may contaminate smoked fish, are easily killed, provided the smoking process is properly done. Therefore, smoked fish should be purchased from a reliable source through a reputable vendor. The spores of the type E can germinate at refrigerator temperature if given time. To provide extra protection, fish harvested from suspect waters may be frozen after it has been smoked.

Principles of Control

1. Purchase smoked fish from a reputable dealer.
2. Use fish promptly, unless frozen. Keep unfrozen smoked fish under strict refrigeration; keep frozen fish solidly frozen.
3. Use frozen smoked fish promptly after it has thawed.

STAPHYLOCOCCUS (STAPH) FOOD POISONING— A FOOD INTOXICATION

This type of food poisoning occurs very frequently. The cause is the toxin of *Staphylococcus aureus* (Table 1). Usually, the victim of this

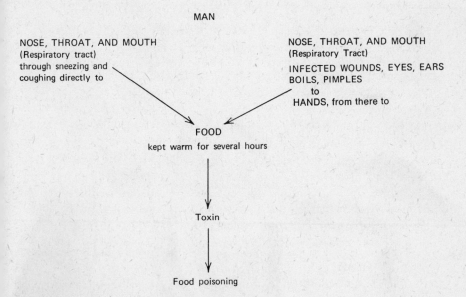

Figure 10. Sources and routes of staphylococci.

Figure 11. NO! (Reprinted by permission of Edward Arnold Publ. Co., London, 1968.)

poisoning becomes ill rather soon after eating the toxic food. He becomes nauseated, vomits, and is plagued by violent intestinal cramps and diarrhea. For details, see Table V, Appendix.

Source and Routes. The most important source of staphylococci capable of causing food poisoning is the human body (Figure 10). Even healthy persons carry these bacteria in their mouths, throats, and noses. Infected wounds are particularly rich in food-poisoning staph, and so are pimples, furuncles, infected throats, eyes, ears, sinuses, and other pus-containing sores.

The organisms get into food if the food handler does not exercise care; for example, when he coughs and sneezes over or near food, or into his hands without washing them afterwards, or into his handkerchief without washing his hands afterwards; or when he picks his nose while preparing food (Figure 11), scratches his face, or picks pimples; or when he has an infected sore on his hands, even *if* he should try to protect it with a bandage.

Food most frequently involved in food poisoning are:

1. *Protein foods* and dishes made with them. Protein foods are meat, milk, poultry, eggs, fish and shellfish.
   The reason: Staph thrive in these items because of their composition and lack of acidity.

2. *Foods that are handled much,* as in grinding, slicing, deboning, shaping.
   The reason: The handling gives the staph a good opportunity to get into the food either directly from the food handler or indirectly from soiled tables and other working surfaces, soiled equipment and utensils, soiled clothing, and the like.
3. *Food that remain for hours in the temperature DANGER ZONE (45-140°F) at which bacterial growth is possible.* This may happen when food stands around the kitchen during preparation hours; when it is forgotten overnight; when it cools slowly; and when it is held on steamtables that do not keep the food hot. (The staph bacteria are able to multiply between 44° and 114°F.)

Can the staphylococci be killed by heating the food?

We can kill staph in food that is heated to 165°F or higher. Unfortunately, such heat treatment is impractical, or even impossible, for many menu items (see Part III-F). Moreover, the toxin that the staph release into the food while multiplying is resistant to heat and cannot be rendered harmless by heating. Therefore, we must:

(a) Keep the food clean and prevent its contamination in the first place.
(b) Keep the food either hot (140°F and higher) or keep it cold (45°F and lower) to prevent multiplication of the staph and the formation of toxin.
(c) Cool food rapidly to safe temperatures.

Principles of Control

1. Persons suffering from respiratory ailments or pus-containing body sores should not handle food (see Part III-D).
2. Food handlers should practice personal cleanliness (see Part II-D).
3. Food handlers should have clean working habits and wash their hands after touching their body and everything else that is likely to be contaminated with staph (see Part III-D).
4. Food should be manipulated with utensils rather than hands, whenever feasible (see Part III-D).
5. Food preparation equipment and utensils must be maintained in a sanitary condition at all times (see Part III-B).
6. Food should not be held at lukewarm temperatures for longer than a couple of hours. Formation of bacterial toxins must be prevented by keeping food either hot or cold. Staph toxin, once formed, is resistant to heat and can *not* be rendered harmless by heating the food.

SALMONELLA FOOD INFECTION OR SALMONELLOSIS

Salmonella food infections (Table 1) are very common. Many species of *Salmonella* can cause salmonellosis.

In contrast to the organisms causing botulism and staph poisoning, the salmonellae do not release toxins into the food in which they multiply. When a person consumes food that contains *Salmonella* bacteria in high numbers, these bacteria cause an infection in the gastrointestinal tract of the victim. *Salmonella* infection causes violent upsets similar to those caused by staph. The symptoms appear, in general, somewhat later than the symptoms of staph poisoning. It may be many hours after the food is eaten or as much as several days, before symptoms appear. The symptoms are nausea, vomiting, diarrhea, abdominal cramps, and weakness. For additional detailed information, see Table VI, Appendix.

A person who has recovered from salmonellosis may remain a carrier for varying lengths of time.

Sources and Routes. There are many sources (Figure 12); important ones are:

1. The intestinal tract of humans.
2. Human wastes—feces and sewage.
3. The intestinal tract of animals.
4. Animal wastes—feces and manure.
5. Food items already contaminated with salmonellae when delivered to the premises of the food service establishment; meat and poultry are examples of sources of salmonellae in the kitchen.

Source 1. The intestinal tract of humans contains salmonellae when a person is ill with salmonellosis. Also, the intestinal tract of persons recovering from a bout with salmonellosis may harbor salmonellae for varying lengths of time; these persons are carriers. When an ill person or a carrier handles food, the salmonellae he harbors may first contaminate his hands, which in turn contaminate the food. Hands may become contaminated with feces when a person visits the toilet. Thorough washing will remove a great number of contaminants. These are important questions:

(a)   Are hands thoroughly washed each time?

(b)   Are soap, plenty of hot water, paper towels provided and used?

Removing contaminants effectively may be difficult when the salmonellae are present in great numbers and/or when the skin of the hands is rough and the nails long. Therefore,

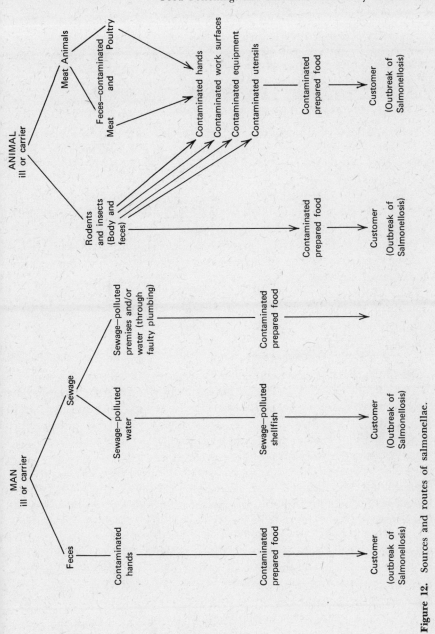

Figure 12. Sources and routes of salmonellae.

(a) *No person while ill with salmonellosis or while a carrier should handle food.*

(b) *Every food handler should thoroughly wash his hands after visiting the toilet.*

(c) *Adequate hand-washing facilities must be provided.*

(d) *The food handler should keep his nails trimmed and clean.*

Source 2. Sewage contains the bacteria present in the human intestinal tract. Sewage in turn may contaminate water and soil, and food harvested from contaminated water and soil. A good example is contaminated shellfish that has been harvested from sewage-polluted waters.

Source 3. The intestinal tract of many animals contains salmonellae at one time or another. Among these animals are cattle, horses, hogs, poultry, dogs, cats, mice, rats, flies, and cockroaches.

Rodents, flies, and cockroaches contaminate food with their *Salmonella*-infested droppings. These animals feed on *Salmonella*-contaminated filth and carry salmonellae on their bodies.

Dogs and cats that may accidentally enter the food preparation area are a menace there. Pets clean themselves by licking, and their tongues become contaminated with salmonellae and other microorganisms of an undesirable nature.

Source 4. Food contaminated with salmonellae when they are received at the food service premises can be an important source of these organisms in the kitchen. A great variety of foodstuffs have been found to be contaminated with salmonellae. Quite frequently contaminated are meat and meat products, and poultry and poultry products. When cattle, hogs, and poultry are slaughtered, the meat may become contaminated with salmonellae during processing.

In the past, processed eggs (such as frozen and dried eggs) have, at times, been found contaminated with salmonella. This is being corrected by killing off the salmonellae through pasteurization of the egg mass before it is frozen or dried. Cracked shell eggs or severely cracked eggs may contain salmonellae. This is why the practice of buying cracked "bargain" eggs is a very poor—in fact, dangerous—practice that is on the "No" list.

Shellfish harvested from polluted waters must be expected to be contaminated with salmonellae. Shellfish should come from safe sources certified by state agencies to be wholesome.

The salmonellae from a contaminated food supply may in turn contaminate prepared food items directly, or they may first contaminate hands, equipment, and utensils that then pass on the salmonellae to prepared food. Figure 12 depicts the direct and indirect sources of salmonellae.

Foods most frequently involved in outbreaks of salmonella food infection:

1. Meats and poultry.
   The reason: These foods are likely to be contaminated when purchased and are therefore especially hazardous.
2. Cracked eggs.
   The reason: The eggs contain salmonellae.
3. Menu items made with meat, milk, poultry, eggs, fish, and shellfish.
   The reason: The salmonellae thrive well in these items because of their composition and lack of acidity.
4. Foods that remained for hours in the temperature DANGER ZONE (45 to 140°F) of bacterial growth.
   The reason: The salmonellae are able to multiply between 44 and 114°F.

Can the salmonellae be killed by heating the food?

We can kill salmonellae by heating contaminated food to 165°F or higher. As is true for staphylococci, we cannot rely on this measure for all items except for certain specific cases to be discussed later on (see Part III-E, F). It is therefore necessary to prevent contamination with salmonellae during food preparation; and to prevent those salmonellae that may be present in the food from multiplying by practicing strict time-temperature control during preparation, service, and storage. Keep food hot (140°F and above) or cold (45°F and below). Cool it rapidly to safe temperatures.

Principles of Control

1. Persons suffering and/or recovering from salmonellosis, or who are carriers, must not handle food.
2. All food handlers must thoroughly wash their hands after visiting the toilet.
3. Food handlers must wash their hands after working with raw meats and poultry and before touching other food, particularly cooked items.
4. Food handlers should have separate work surfaces for raw and cooked foods, to avoid cross contamination.
5. Food handlers should prevent cross contamination. If the same work surfaces have to be used for raw and cooked foods, the surfaces must be thoroughly scrubbed and sanitized before they are used for cooked food. Remember this when disjointing raw meat or poultry

on a work surface, then using the same surface for deboning and slicing the cooked meat.

6. Plumbing must be kept in excellent working order to prevent sewage from contaminating water and food.

7. Rodents and insects must be kept under strict control.

8. Pets must not be allowed in the areas where food is handled.

9. Meat and poultry should be government-inspected; shellfish should be certified to be wholesome; cracked eggs should not be used.

10. All equipment and utensils should be kept in an excellent condition of repair and cleanliness.

11. Excellent housekeeping should be practiced throughout the establishment.

12. Strict time-temperature control should be practiced during actual food preparation, hot-holding, and cooling. Keep food hot (140°F and above) or cold (45°F and below); cool hot food rapidly.

PERFRINGENS FOOD POISONING

Perfringens food poisoning (Table 1) was not well understood or recognized until fairly recently. It seems possible that the illness produced by the organism is caused by a toxin. Scientists would need to prove this, however.

The symptoms of the illness are similar to those of staph poisoning and *Salmonella* infection, but they are less violent.

The organism causing the illness is *Clostridium perfringens,* a spore-former that grows best without air; it grows well at warm temperatures, above 100°F. (See also Table VII, Appendix).

The source of the organism is the intestinal tract of humans and animals (Figure 13). Consequently, it is also found in feces, sewage, manure, and soil. Kitchen dust is a rich source of the spores; in fact, the organism seems to be everywhere.

Being of intestinal origin, the organism has a good chance to contaminate meat after slaughter.

What foods are most frequently involved?

Most frequently indicted are meat and meat gravy, beef and veal being at the top of the list of offenders.

Examples of circumstances frequently associated with perfringens poisoning are these:

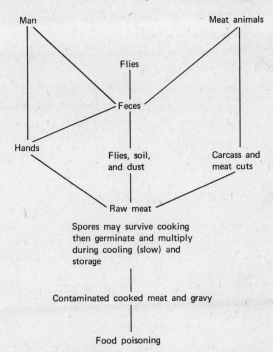

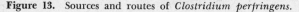

Figure 13.   Sources and routes of *Clostridium perfringens.*

(a) Meat and gravy were held warm for hours at temperatures *below* that recommended for hot-holding, which is 140°F or higher.

(b) Meat was cooked in advance and cooled slowly, and while cooling, the meat and gravy were actually in the DANGER ZONE for many hours.

(c) Gravy was held overnight on the back of the stove, neither hot nor cold.

(d) Cooked meat was recontaminated: meat was placed on table or board or other working surface on which raw meat had been handled previously and which was superficially cleaned or not cleaned at all. Or meat was sliced on a superficially-cleaned slicer or with another unclean utensil.

Are the spores killed in routine cooking of meat?

Unfortunately, there are many strains of this bacterium around, and some are very resistant to heat. We cannot rely on heating to kill the pathogen; we must prevent its multiplication. To do this successfully, we need to know the conditions under which multiplication can occur.

1. Growth of *Clostridium perfringens* can take place between 60 and 122°F.
2. Growth is excellent between 109 and 116°F. These temperatures are dangerously close to those at which cooked meat is frequently held warm to prevent it from getting overdone before it is served.

Consequently, the most important control measure against perfringens food poisoning are (a) cleanliness and (b) strict time-temperature control.

Principles of Control

1. Food handlers must prevent contamination of cooked food with *Clostridium perfringens* by using separate work surfaces for raw and cooked meats; if this is not feasible, they must thoroughly clean work surfaces after they have been used for raw meat.
2. Food handlers must wash their hands after working with raw meat and before handling cooked food.
3. The food-preparation area should be kept as free of dust as is feasible.
4. Meat slicers and other meat-cutting utensils must be properly cleaned after use.
5. Food handlers must thoroughly wash their hands after visiting the toilet and each time they pick up articles from the floor, lace their shoes, or handle crates, packages, and any other articles likely to be soiled.
6. Strict time-temperature control must be practiced in the preparation, hot-holding, and cooling of meat and gravy. Meat and gravy must be held hot (140°F or higher) or cold (45°F or lower), and cooling of hot food should proceed rapidly.

STREPTOCOCCUS FOOD INFECTION

Streptococcus food infections seem to be rare. They are suspected to be caused by several species of a group of streptococci known as fecal streptococci. These cocci are inhabitants of the intestinal tracts of humans and animals.

Meat and poultry may become contaminated with fecal streptococci during slaughter and packing operations. The presence of these streptococci in the kitchen may also stem from the human source, namely, unwashed hands contaminated with feces.

Large numbers of fecal streptococci must evidently be present i\
in order to cause symptoms of poisoning in the victim.

The symptoms of *Streptococcus* food infection are rather mild. They\
sist of nausea and sometimes vomiting and coliclike pains of the abdom_ii.

Which foods and what circumstances of food handling have been associated
with streptococcus food infections?

Meats, especially tenderized hams, have been involved; the fecal streptococci are able to grow in salty food. Other foods indicted are poultry,
cream-filled pastry, and a variety of prepared menu items.

The circumstances associated with *Streptococcus* food infections are,
primarily, poor temperature control—namely, keeping perishable food
within the DANGER ZONE for too long. The fecal streptococci can grow
over a wide range of temperatures, from 42 to 126°F.

Principles of Control

1. Tenderized hams must be kept under strict refrigeration.
2. Food handlers must practice excellent personal hygiene and thoroughly wash their hands after visiting the toilet.
3. Sanitary food-preparation methods are essential; after working with
   raw meat and before handling other food items, food handlers must
   wash their hands and thoroughly clean work surfaces and equipment.
4. Strict time-temperature control is required during preparation, hot-
   holding, and cooling of prepared foods. Keep food hot (140°F and
   above) or cold (45°F and below); cool hot food rapidly to safe temperatures.

SECTION D

Food Poisoning Caused by Agents Other than Microorganisms

Poisonous plants, poisonous animals, poisonous chemicals added to food, and metals from unsuitable cooking utensils, have all been reported as causes of food poisoning.

Poisonous Plants and Animals

Certain mushrooms are poisonous, but mushrooms purchased from a reliable vendor are safe.

Green potatoes and sprouting potatoes have been reported to cause food poisoning. However, there is little basis for these claims, since at least 17 pounds of green potatoes would have to be eaten at one sitting to cause poisoning. For extra protection, however, sprouts, eyes, and any green portion of the potato skin should be removed when sprouted or green potatoes must be used. Refuse to accept such potatoes upon delivery.

Other plants that have been reported to cause food poisoning are not mentioned here, as these plants are not used in preparing food for the public. The interested reader is referred to Dr. Dack's book on food poisoning (see Readings, Part II).

Among animals that have been reported to cause poisoning are ocean mussels and clams, from certain regions within the United States and Canada, that had fed on poisonous plankton (plankton are tiny ocean plants and animals that float in the water and serve as food to shellfish). However, seafood from approved waters is safe. The widespread notion that shellfish should not be eaten during the months *not* containing the letter "r" is false. It originated at a time of poor refrigeration during the warm months of the year.

Poisoning by Chemicals

Chemical poisoning often acts within minutes. Fortunately this type of poisoning is uncommon in an orderly food-service establishment. Most

48

cases are caused by negligence and disorder in the food-service department —for example, when cleaning compounds, polishes, insecticides, and the like are stored together with food-preparation ingredients, or are not labeled, or both, and thus are mistakenly used for food ingredients. There is no excuse for slipshod housekeeping.

Chemicals must be stored separately in closed, clearly labeled containers, away from the area where food is stored and prepared.

Chemicals that are used on fruits and vegetables to keep them free from plant and insect diseases should not cause food poisoning. These chemicals are applied according to schedules that in general ensure that they do not adhere to the food in injurious amounts at harvesting time. For extra protection, it is recommended that *all fruits and vegetables be carefully washed before they are used.*

Metals may get into food by the use of food-preparation and storage utensils unsuitable for this purpose. The following metals have been reported to cause food poisoning: cadmium, antimony, lead, zinc, and occasionally copper.

Cadmium, when employed as plating material for ice-cube trays, refrigerator shelves, and syrup pumps, has been reported to cause poisoning. Antimony, which occurs as an impurity in grey enamelware, and zinc, which is used in galvanized containers, may render acid food poisonous. Copper has been reported to cause poisoning when in prolonged contact with acid foods and carbonated beverages.

Containers, shelves, and pipes containing the above materials may present hazards from poisoning, especially when used with acid food and drink.

Lead is condemned for plating purposes. When used in solder, lead must be kept to a low percentage. The health authorities should be consulted about applicable regulations.

SECTION E

Reporting and Investigating
Foodborne Illnesses

One important means of preventing future incidences in outbreaks of foodborne illness is to learn from the mistakes of the past. Therefore, we must trace all incidences to their causes. The food service manager does not possess the technical know-how that a sanitarian and a bacteriologist have; therefore, he needs the help of the health authorities in tracing the cause of the incident and in correcting the situation to prevent reoccurrence.

Reporting to the health authorities a food-poisoning outbreak, or the suspicion of one, should be prompt. Delay in reporting not only severely hampers the investigation, but may also allow the illness to spread. In some states reporting is required by law; in others it is voluntary. Consult your local health authorities.

Whether reporting is compulsory or not, it is strongly recommended that all suspected cases of foodborne illness be reported to the health authorities; they can be of tremendous help to management in preventing future incidences.

The investigation of an outbreak of foodborne illness seeks to accomplish these tasks:

(a) Find which meal and specific menu item caused the illness.

(b) Determine the organism or other agent that caused the outbreak.

(c) Determine where and how the food became contaminated.

(d) Determine the opportunity for bacterial multiplication in the food.

To do this, a team of investigators will question the victims, and visit the food service establishment to interview management and employees, to take samples of suspected menu items if they are still available and to check on the sanitary condition of the operation.

Since many food-poisoning organisms are harbored in the human body, the persons who prepared the suspected meal—or menu items—are examined to detect acute or recent illness and the presence of carriers. Specimens may be taken from food handlers to detect the possible presence of food-poisoning bacteria in and on their bodies.

Swabs are also taken from surfaces of tables, cutting blocks, and other food-preparation equipment to determine whether they are contaminated, and with what organisms or poison.

Food samples, specimens taken from food handlers, and swabs taken from equipment, are handed over to a laboratory for examination. All information is organized in a report.

It is extremely important that management and every employee interviewed cooperate to the fullest with the health authorities in their endeavor to clarify the causes of the incident. The health authorities will have valuable suggestions to make as to what needs to be done to remedy the situation and to avoid a repetition of similar incidents in the future.

What have past investigations taught us?

Of the outbreaks reported, very few are waterborne and milkborne, while over 90% are foodborne (Figure 14). Among the outbreaks caused by food, the chief offenders are poultry, meat, and fishery products. Staphylococci and salmonellae are the most frequent causes. Mishandling of food by unclean personnel with unclean equipment in an unclean environment, and long exposure of food to warm temperatures, are most frequently the circumstances associated with outbreaks.

What types of food-service establishments are involved in outbreaks of foodborne illnesses?

The answer is, all kinds. Public eating establishments top the listing of reported outbreaks, but schools, colleges, social gatherings, camps, private clubs, nursing homes, and hospitals have been involved also.

Recommendations for the manager to follow:

1. Invite the local department of health to participate in your sanitation program. Solicit their advice; ask them to speak before your employees on matters of sanitary food handling. Do everything to create a feeling of "being in this business of sanitation together."
2. Seek the advice and cooperation of the health authorities in all matters of health and sanitation *before* an outbreak of foodborne illness has occurred in your establishment. Outbreaks can be prevented by appropriate sanitary food management. The health authorities will help you to assess your operation for sanitation.

Figure 14. Comparative incidence of foodborne illness caused by water, milk and other food.

3. Retain a small sample of every menu item served each day, under refrigeration, for 24 to 48 hours. Then, if an outbreak of food poisoning should occur, the establishment can prove or disprove the charge.

4. Notify the health authorities promptly in case of an outbreak or suspected outbreak and save a sample of every menu item for analysis.

5. Cooperate fully with the investigating team; give information freely, and stimulate your employees to do the same.

SECTION F

Important Facts in Brief for Part II

- Spoilage commonly refers to food decomposition and other damage that interferes with food quality and renders food unfit to eat.
- Spoiled food does not necessarily present a hazard from a public-health point of view, but spoiled food should be regarded as suspect. Spoilage may cause heavy financial losses to the food-service business. Spoilage indicates poor management.
- Disease transmission refers to the fact that germs causing communicable diseases may be passed on from one person to others by way of food.
- Food transmitting disease germs never appears spoiled.
- Transmission may be direct from person to food to person; or it may be indirect. Important in-between vehicles of transmission are sewage, sewage-polluted water, rodents and insects.
- The source of the human pathogens that are frequently transmitted through food is a person's body, in particular his respiratory and intestinal tract.
- The persons most likely to transmit disease-producing germs to food and eventually to the customer are the food handlers; they are the persons who prepare the food, serve it, and clean the food-preparation and eating utensils. Therefore, persons who are ill with communicable diseases or are carriers are a menace in the food-service establishment.
- Carriers can be particularly dangerous because they do not look or feel ill and are likely to report to work. Carriers are known to have infected large numbers of customers before being detected as carriers.
- Certain germs causing animal diseases can be transmitted through food to man and cause disease in man.
- Bacterial food poisoning and food infections are caused by consuming food containing bacterial toxins or high numbers of certain infectious bacteria. Symptoms following the consumption of the offending food are violent nausea, vomiting, abdominal cramps, diarrhea, and general weakness. Foods become poisonous or infectious because they are mishandled.

They usually look, smell, and taste like wholesome food and do not give the appearance of being spoiled. Organisms most frequently responsible for food poisoning and food infections are staphylococci, salmonellae, and perfringens bacteria.

Most of these organisms come originally from the body of humans and animals. With proper sanitary care their entry into food can and must be controlled at all stages of food preparations; and their multiplication in food can and must be prevented through strict control of time and temperature.

Here are the rules: Keep food clean, and either hot or cold. Cool warm food quickly to safe temperatures. Application of these rules requires the cooperation of everyone in the establishment. Sanitation is everyone's responsibility every minute of the day and every day of the year.

General control measures to prevent food spoilage, disease transmission and food poisoning are:

(a) Purchase a sound food supply from reliable sources and use sanitary storage procedures.

(b) Provide and maintain an adequate, clean facility: clean kitchen, dry storage, refrigerators, and freezers; clean locker rooms and toilets; clean garbage disposal; and effective and safe rodent and insect control.

(c) Provide and maintain adequate, clean, food-preparation equipment and utensils and sanitary eating and drinking utensils.

(d) Employ healthy food handlers and continuously train them to be health-conscious, personally clean, and eager to maintain good sanitary standards in their work.

(e) Use sanitary procedures aimed at preventing bacterial contamination of food during actual preparation, holding, and service. Maintain effective control of time and temperature at every stage of preparation, hot-holding, cooling, and serving of the food.

(f) Be convinced that sanitation is important; set high sanitary standards, emphasizing their importance to employees and seeing to it that these standards are constantly maintained.

Detailed control measures will be discussed in Part III.

Study Questions for Part II

1. Define spoilage of fresh foods.
2. What are signs of spoilage of canned foods? Explain.
3. State the difference between disease transmission and food poisoning.
4. Name some very important diseases that have been known to be transmitted through food.
5. What are some important routes by which pathogens are transmitted from man to prepared food? Explain.
6. What is a carrier and what is his role in disease transmission? Explain.
7. Explain the meaning of food intoxication and food infection. Give examples of each.
8. Define time-temperature control of foods.
9. Define potentially hazardous foods.

Readings for Part II

Dack, Gail M. *Food Poisoning*. 3rd ed. University of Chicago Press, Chicago, Ill. 1956.

Frazier, William C. *Food Microbiology*. 2nd ed. McGraw-Hill Book Co., New York. 1967. Part II-11, III, V, VI.

Hobbs, Betty. *Food Poisoning and Food Hygiene*. 2nd ed. Edward Arnold Ltd., London. 1968. Part I.

Longrée, Karla. *Quantity Food Sanitation*. 2nd ed. Wiley-Interscience, a division of John Wiley and Sons, Inc., New York. 1972. Chapters I, III, IV, V, VI. VII.

Riemann, H., Editor. *Food-Borne Infections and Intoxications*. Food Science and Technology Series. Academic Press, New York. 1969.

U.S. Department of Health, Education and Welfare, Public Health Service. *Food Service Sanitation Manual,* including a Model Food Service Sanitation Ordinance and Code. PHS Publ. No. 934, Washington, D.C. 1962.

U.S. Department of Health, Education and Welfare, Public Health Service. *Salmonellosis*. PHS Publ. No. 1262, Washington, D.C. 1965.

U.S. Department of Health, Education and Welfare, Public Health Service. *Botulism*. PHS Publ. No. 999-FP-1, Cincinnati, Ohio. 1964.

West, B. B., Levelle Wood, and Virginia Harger. *Food Service in Institutions*. 4th ed. John Wiley and Sons, Inc., New York. 1965. Sections II-9, III-11.

Wogan, Gerald, W., Editor. *Mycotoxins in Food-Stuffs*. MIT Press, Cambridge, Mass. 1965.

PART III

Sanitary Practice

SECTION A

Clean Facility (Physical Plant)

The physical plant of a food service operation refers to:

1. Kitchens and all other areas where food is prepared, stored, and served.
2. Areas where equipment is washed and stored.
3. The dressing or locker rooms for employees, and toilet rooms.
4. The area for garbage disposal.

Sanitation of the physical plant involves:

1. Cleanability of walls, floors, and ceilings due to good construction, smooth materials, and good state of repair.
2. Proper sewage disposal and plumbing; presence of floor drains where needed because of spillage or method of cleaning floor.
3. Good ventilation.
4. Good lighting.
5. Adequate hand-washing facilities.
6. Sanitary dressing rooms or locker rooms and sanitary toilet facilities.
7. Sanitary garbage disposal.
8. Control of rodents and insects.
9. Separate storage area for cleaning materials and utensils.
10. Regular and adequate cleaning of facility.

Cleanability of Walls, Floors, and Ceilings

Walls, floors, and ceilings should be constructed so as to be easy to clean. They should have smooth, hard surfaces, which are easy to clean (whereas rough and absorbent ones are not).

Walls, floors, and ceilings must be maintained in a good state of repair, since surfaces in poor repair are impossible to keep clean. Rough surfaces and surfaces with rough and open places collect debris, grime, and dust, and provide harboring places for vermin, such as cockroaches. Cracks may

59

provide entry places for rats and mice. Therefore, cracks must be sealed, and rough surfaces changed to smooth, cleanable ones.

Adequate Sewage Disposal and Plumbing

Sewage Disposal. Improper sewage disposal can cause, and has caused, serious illness and outbreaks of food poisoning. Sewage contains dangerous germs, and must never be allowed to contaminate food or equipment and the area where food is stored or prepared.

Improper sewage disposal can:

1. Pollute the water.
2. Pollute food through overhead leakage of pipes.
3. Contaminate equipment.
4. Attract flies and other insects; these insects, in turn, contaminate food.

Sewage must be disposed of in a manner satisfactory to the health authorities, which means that sewage must be directed into:

1. A public sewage system.
2. A sewage system that is constructed and operated according to the rules and regulations of the health authorities; consult these.

Plumbing. Improper plumbing is a hazard for these reasons:

1. Cross connections between pipes carrying drinking water and pipes carrying nondrinking water.
2. Drainage stoppage.
3. Overhead leakage.
4. Backflow of sewage into drains from refrigerators, drains, dishwasher drains, etc.

All plumbing must be installed and maintained in a manner satisfactory to the health authorities. Plumbing must be maintained in good working condition, and any malfunction such as leakage, stoppage and flooding, should be reported by employees to the supervisor or manager so that the hazard can be corrected at once.

Floor Drains. Floor drains should be provided in all areas where water is spilled on the floor during normal operations or where floors are cleaned by hosing. State, city, and county health departments may have special regulations regarding floor drains. Consult your local health authorities.

Floor drains must be kept in good operating condition. When stoppage occurs, the supervisor or manager should be informed and the condition corrected at once.

Ventilation

Kitchens, storerooms, dishwashing rooms, dining rooms, locker or dressing rooms, toilets, and storage rooms for garbage and rubbish should be well ventilated. Ventilation systems should be installed and maintained in a manner satisfactory to the health authority. Examples of ventilation systems are window exhaust fans, hood exhaust systems, unit blowers, and unit cooling systems.

What proper ventilation can do:

1. Chase out air that has become hot, stale, odorous, moist, greasy, smoky, and the like, because of cooking, dishwashing, and various other causes.
2. Prevent deposit of droplets of moisture on walls and ceilings. Moisture furthers growth of microorganisms. Droplets containing bacteria and mold may fall onto food and food-preparation surfaces and equipment and contaminate these.

Lighting

Good lighting is particularly needed in these areas:

1. Kitchens—in order to prepare food in a sanitary manner.
2. Food storage rooms—in order to recognize the condition of the food, to avoid spills, and to facilitate cleaning.
3. Areas where pots, pans and utensils are washed—to see that these get clean.
4. Areas where hands are washed—to see that hands and nails get clean.
5. Dressing or locker rooms—to see that the whole person looks tidy and clean.
6. Toilets—to see that they are in a sanitary condition and to facilitate cleaning.
7. Storage areas for rubbish and garbage—to check on orderliness, cleanliness, and freedom from vermin.

With good lighting, dirt becomes more conspicuous. With poor lighting, good cleaning is impossible.

Adequate Hand-Washing Facilities

Responsibility of management:

1. Hand-washing facilities should be made available in several locations. Several states have legal specifications regarding hand-washing facilities. Since hands are the most important sources of germs with which food becomes contaminated, management should provide hand-wash-

ing facilities in locations where hands are likely to become contaminated with dangerous germs:

(a)   Adjacent to toilet rooms.

(b)   In locker or dressing rooms.

(c)   In areas where food is prepared.

No employee will walk great distances to wash hands every time these should be washed. Therefore, *hand-washing facilities should be placed conveniently and be made available in adequate numbers.* They should be installed so as to satisfy the requirements of the health authority.

2.   Hand-washing facilities should consist of:

(a)   A wash bowl equipped with hot and cold (or tempered) water.

(b)   Liquid or powdered soap or detergent.

(c)   Individual towels or other hand-drying devices such as air dryers.

3.   Maintenance should be meticulous. The wash bowls, dispensers for soap, and other drying devices should be regularly and thoroughly cleaned. Soap and towels should be checked and replenished *before* they run out.

Dressing or Locker Rooms and Toilet Facilities

Responsibility of management:

1.   *Dressing rooms or locker rooms* should be available so food service personnel may change their clothes and store their belongings. Street clothes can be a source of undesirable bacteria and should not be worn or hung in the kitchen. Also, clothes should not be hung in storerooms or toilets. Dressing or locker rooms should be located outside the areas where food is prepared, stored, and served. Uniforms should not be worn outside the food-service establishment. Dressing or locker rooms should be well screened and provided with proper hand-washing facilities. Mirrors should be hung away from hand-washing facilities.

Dressing or locker rooms should be kept in a sanitary condition at all times. They must be scheduled for regular and thorough cleaning. Floors and wash bowls should be cleaned daily.

2.   *Toilet facilities* should be provided in areas separate from those where food is prepared, stored, and served. Toilet rooms should be well screened and have tight-fitting and self-closing doors. Toilet rooms and facilities (such as commodes and urinals) should be kept clean and in good repair. Toilet tissue should be available at all times. Receptacles should be available for waste materials and should be emptied frequently, at least once a day.

3.   Hand-washing facilities should be available in or next to dressing

rooms and toilet rooms and should include washbowls, a hot and cold or tempered water supply, soap, and towels or air dryers. It is of utmost importance that everyone wash his hands after visiting the toilet. Signs should be posted as a reminder. The Health Department will furnish the signs upon request.

Washrooms must be immaculately maintained: floors, washbowls and mirrors cleaned daily; and soap and towels checked and replenished, if necessary. SOAP AND TOWELS MUST BE AVAILABLE AT ALL TIMES.

The responsibilities of employees are to:

It is the responsibility of everyone to keep dressing or locker rooms, toilets, and washrooms tidy and clean.

1. Put your clothes away neatly.
2. Don't leave articles around or clutter up space that ought to be available to everyone.
3. Don't comb your hair over the washbowl, creating a disgusting mess.
4. Keep toilet seats clean.
5. Thoroughly wash your hands after dressing and after visiting the toilet.
6. Report to your supervisor any disfunctioning of equipment or lack of toilet tissue, soap, and towels.
7. Cooperate to the fullest with fellow employees and management to keep areas neat and clean. Clean up after yourself and leave these places in a condition in which you would hope to find them yourself.

Sanitary Garbage Disposal

Improperly disposed garbage is a nuisance as well as a source of danger to sanitation. Unpleasant odors are a nuisance. The real dangers of *improperly* stored garbage are these:

(a) It becomes a harboring place for vermin such as rats, mice, flies and cockroaches.
(b) It represents a source of contamination of food and of equipment and utensils used in food preparation.
(c) It makes good housekeeping a difficult, if not impossible, task.

The responsibilities of management are to:

1. Provide garbage containers of durable materials that do not leak and do not absorb liquids; and provide them in numbers sufficient to hold all the garbage and other refuse between collections. Cans kept outside should sit on a rack (Figure 15).

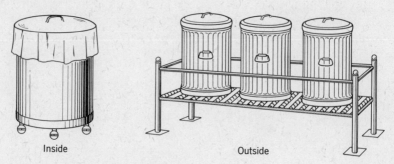

Inside   Outside

Figure 15. Sanitary disposal of refuse.

2. Provide either tight-fitting covers for the cans or a special, enclosed, vermin-proof, cool garbage room. A refrigerated garbage room aids in preventing rapid decay of garbage and the development of bad odors resulting from decay.
3. After cans are emptied, have them thoroughly cleaned inside and out; provide brushes, detergent, and plenty of hot water for the job. In large operations, steam-cleaning devices or can-washing machines may be available.
4. Have the storage area for garbage cleaned regularly and frequently.
5. Check frequently for signs of vermin activity.
6. Install mechanical disposers (Figure 16) to reduce the amount of garbage and the number of unsightly garbage cans.

The responsibilities of employees are to:

1. Avoid spilling garbage and clean up spills if they happen.
2. Replace lids on cans after these have been opened.
3. Carefully close doors of the garbage rooms to shut out vermin.
4. Report to supervisors any signs of vermin activity.
5. Do a thorough job of cleaning the cans and the storage area for garbage.

Control of Rodents and Insects

The presence of rodents such as rats and mice, and insects such as flies and cockroaches, is a menace to a food-service operation. Rodents and insects may transmit disease by contaminating food and food-preparation equipment and utensils. Their entry into the establishment must be prevented (Figure 17), and specimens present must be killed.

The responsibilities of management are:

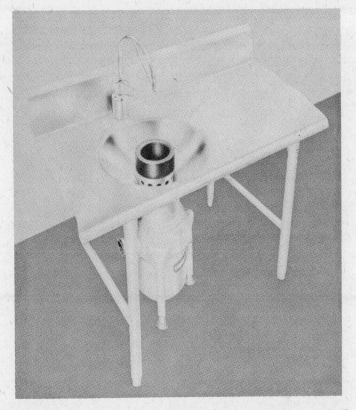

Figure 16. Mechanical waste disposer. (Reprinted from B. B. West et al., *Food Service in Institutions,* 4th ed., 1966, by permission of John Wiley & Sons, New York.)

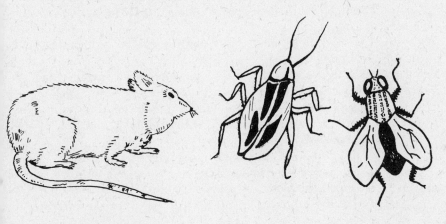

Figure 17. Keep them out!

1. *To keep out flies by:*
   (a) Having all windows and doors screened and by protecting other openings to the outside.
   (b) Providing screened storage for garbage.
   (c) Providing clean, ventilated, well screened toilets.
2. *To control cockroaches by:*
   (a) Having all openings in ceilings, walls, and floors sealed.
   (b) Having damp areas eliminated, such as overflows, drippings from drains, and leaks from pipes; and crevices around equipment and pipes.
   (c) Having all incoming boxes of foodstuffs inspected for presence of roaches and to refuse roach-infested goods.
   (d) Inspecting kitchens, storage rooms, and garbage rooms frequently for the presence of vermin. Remember that cockroaches are night insects that come out of hiding at darkness. Signs of cockroaches are their droppings, which, when dry, look like mouse pellets but possess lengthwise ridges and a musty odor.
   (e) Hiring a professional exterminator for regular chemical control of vermin.
   (f) Having the premises cleaned every night so that no crumbs and bits of food are left as food for vermin.
   (g) Having the premises inspected every night for left-out food.
3. *To control rodents by:*
   (a) Rodent-proofing the building. All openings to outside should be protected against the entrance of rats and mice; to do this properly, the services of a professional are recommended. Rodents may squeeze through very small openings. A crack $\frac{1}{2}''$ wide will admit an adult mouse or a young rat. Doors should be self-closing.
   (b) Exterminating rodents, by using the services of a professional exterminator.
   (c) Keeping constant watch for signs of rodents' presence and activities. Signs of mice are their droppings ($\frac{1}{4}''$ in size) and gnawings on wood and food containers (sacks, crates, cartons); signs of rats are their fairly large pellets ($\frac{1}{2}$ to $\frac{3}{4}''$); their runways (characterized by a smudgy trail); and gnawings.
   (d) Maintaining high standards of cleanliness at all times.
   (e) Inspecting the premises every night for left-out food, open screens, open doors, and other entrances to the outside.
   (f) Inspecting groceries, upon their delivery, for the presence of rodents.

The responsibilities of employees are to:

1. Not leave screen doors and other entrances to the outside open.
2. Replace the covers of garbage cans immediately after emptying the garbage, and close the door to the garbage room when leaving.
3. Clean up spills in kitchen, pantry, dining area, and storerooms immediately and thoroughly.
4. Never leave food unprotected.
5. Never leave food out overnight.
6. Report to supervisor the presence of vermin or signs of the activity of vermin.

Separate Storage Area for Cleaning Materials, Utensils, and Equipment

Cleaners such as detergents, soaps, ammonia, polishes, and other materials must be stored separately, never in the kitchen. Cleaning equipment and utensils (such as vacuum cleaners, brooms, mops, buckets, mop trucks, and the like) must also be stored separately.

The responsibilities of management are to:

1. Provide a separate, well-ventilated and well-lighted janitor area for storing cleaning materials, utensils and equipment.
2. Provide, in the janitor area, a separate sink for drawing water; making up cleaning solutions; washing out mops, sponges and other cleaning utensils; and emptying buckets.
3. Provide racks for drying cleaning utensils.
4. Schedule the area for cleaning.
5. Inspect the area for orderliness and cleanliness.

The responsibilities of employees are to:

1. Report to supervisor when supplies and utensils need replenishing and when equipment requires repair.
2. Keep janitor area orderly and clean.

Regular and Adequate Cleaning of Facility

Cleaning of the food-service facility is a fundamental and important part of the operation. Routine checks are made by inspectors from various county, state, and federal health departments to insure that high standards in sanitation are maintained.

The Purpose of Cleaning is to Remove Soil

Soil is "matter out of place."
Soil or dirt can be dust, grime, grease, food particles, and even bacteria. Types of soil fall in two basic categories:

(a) Soils that water will dissolve; these are the water-soluble soils. Examples are sugar, jelly, fruit juices, and salt.
(b) Soils that water will not dissolve; these are the water-insoluble soils and our most common forms of dirt. Examples are grease, oil dust, food particles, and other solid matter, usually in various combinations.

What is a Clean Surface?

A surface is clean when it is free of soil; it is *bacteriologically clean when the majority of bacteria have been removed by sanitizing* the surface, using hot water or special chemical sanitizers. Therefore, when bacteriological cleanliness is necessary from a public-health point of view, sanitizing must be part of the cleaning operation. Cleaning and sanitizing may be performed in one operation, using special cleaning-sanitizing agents.

How to Clean

The responsibilities of management are to:

1. Set the standards. The local health department will advise a food-service operator what sanitation standards are expected of the establishment.
2. Prepare a cleaning schedule.
3. Train personnel how to clean.
4. Provide adequate cleaning equipment, utensils, and materials.
5. Provide supervision to see that jobs are done properly.

The personnel must be informed regarding:

· What has to be cleaned.
· When a soiled item should be cleaned.
· How it should be cleaned.
· How to keep it clean until next use.

Cleaning Schedule

It would be desirable if one could set up a cleaning schedule applicable to every food-service establishment. This is impossible, since very few food-service operations are alike. Some cleaning is daily routine and should be included in the daily work schedule of the employees. Some cleaning is weekly and should be scheduled on the day when the most employees are available or when the work load is lightest. Special cleaning, which is necessary a few times a year, may require specific scheduling of additional specialized help.

In general, *there should be no large-scale sweeping and cleaning while food is being prepared.* Dry sweeping raises dust, which contaminates the food. Wet sweeping is apt to cause slipperiness and invites accidents. *However, spilled food should be removed from floors immediately,* dry spills by sweeping, wet spills by wiping.

Below is a list that indicates when specific areas should be cleaned. *This represents a minimum cleaning schedule.* Under certain circumstances more frequent cleaning may be necessary.

Daily

1. Floors, at least those of areas where traffic is heavy, as kitchens, bake-shops, pantries, dishwashing rooms, much-used walk-in refrigerators and vestibules, corridors, dining rooms, washrooms, toilet rooms
2. Washbowls in kitchens, washrooms, and locker rooms
3. Hood filters (if fryers and broilers are used daily)

Weekly

1. Floors in areas where traffic is only light. Much-used floors need to be cleaned more frequently, according to use
2. Hood

3. Walk-in refrigerators
4. Platforms
5. Duckboards
6. Garbage rooms
7. Windowsills, transoms

Monthly

1. Windows inside
2. Storerooms

Special

1. Windows outside
2. Walls, unless spattering requires frequent, regular cleaning
3. Light fixtures
4. Venetian blinds
5. Freezers

Directions

Cleaning procedures must be written out as specific directions. Management or other key personnel are responsible for providing these, and employees should be instructed in (1) *the use of cleaning equipment and utensils* and (2) *the use of cleaners.* Stressed should be the importance of using the prescribed cleaners in the prescribed strength for the specific jobs. It is most important to

READ LABELS AND FOLLOW DIRECTIONS AS STATED ON THE CLEANING PRODUCT USED.

Measuring devices should be provided for preparing the solutions exactly as prescribed; employees should also be instructed in (3) *the care of cleaning equipment and utensils after use,* such as the cleaning and drying of buckets, mops, brushes, sponges, cloths, and the like. Cleaning equipment, utensils, and materials must never be stored with food. A special area equipped with water, a sink, and drying racks should be provided where equipment and utensils can be cared for and stored.

Floor Care

Floors require different care according to the material of which they are made.

Some general rules are as follows:

1. Wipe up spills promptly before they are tracked over the floor.
2. Determine the desirable frequency of cleaning; frequency of general cleaning depends on factors such as the extent of traffic and the degree and type of soil. Floors subjected to heavy traffic, food spills, and the like, must be cleaned daily.
3. Hard floors (except wood floors) take flooding with water; examples of hard floors are marble, terrazzo, ceramic tile, and cement floors. Wood floors* made of hard wood are hard floors, but they do not tolerate flooding with water or water-base cleaning solution.
4. Soft floors do not take flooding with water; examples of soft floors are asphalt, linoleum, rubber, tile, and cork.
5. Floors need to be cleaned of gross litter and sticky and caked material and swept before they are wet-cleaned. Use putty knife to remove caked and sticky soil.

Suggestions for the type of cleaner to be used for different floors are given in Table 2.

Broom-Sweeping

Utensils and materials needed:

Long-handled broom
Dust pans and hand brush
Putty knife

Procedure

1. Pick up gross litter; pry up sticky material with a putty knife.
2. Start sweeping where the area is entered.
3. Sweep under and around large pieces of equipment; use a hand brush for areas that cannot be reached with a broom.
4. Do not accumulate dirt in large piles; sweep it into small piles to be picked up later with a counter brush and dustpan.
5. Clean brushes with a coarse (nail) comb. If they are soiled, wash them in water and detergent, rinse and hang up to dry. Clean the dustpan and putty knife.

---

* Wood is no longer used for kitchen floors, but hard woods (oak, birch, and maple) are still being used in dining rooms.

Type of Flooring	Hardness	Where Used	Advantages	Disadvantages	Cleaner
TERRAZZO	Hard marble chips in cement	Kitchen; dining rooms	Durable	Damaged by alkalies; stained by grease unless well sealed	Use mild cleaners; scrub; rinse; mop dry
CERAMIC TILE	Hard		Resists grease stains if glazed; durable	Unglazed tile easily stained by grease; spaces between tile difficult to clean; slippery when wet	Alkaline cleaners are safe; scrub to clean between tiles; rinse; mop dry
CONCRETE	Hard		Durable	Gives off dust; becomes stained by grease unless well sealed	Alkaline cleaners are safe; scrub, rinse (sealing concrete will make it more cleanable)
ASPHALT TILE	Soft	Dining rooms	Durable; nonslippery even when wet	Poor resistance to grease	Mildly alkaline to neutral cleaners; mop; rinse; mop dry
RUBBER TILE	Soft		Durable	Damaged by grease	Mild cleaners; mop; rinse; mop dry; NEVER USE STRONG CLEANERS
VINYL	Soft		Nonslippery even when wet; durable; resistant to grease		Mildly alkaline to neutral cleaner; mop; rinse; mop dry
VINYL ASBESTOS	Soft		Durable; resistant to grease		Alkaline cleaners safe; mop; rinse; mop dry
CORK TILE	Soft			Easily damaged by sharp objects; grease will penetrate unless well sealed	Use special cleaners for cork floors (sealing cork tile makes floors more cleanable)

Dust-Mopping

Dust-mopping raises less dust than broom-sweeping. Dust-mopping is more efficient than broom-sweeping on floors such as wood, asphalt tile, vinyl tile, linoleum, and terazzo, and on floors that have been sealed.
Utensils and materials needed:

Dust mop
Dust pan and hand brush
Putty knife

Procedure

1. Pick up gross litter; pry up sticky material with a putty knife.
2. Move easily movable equipment and furniture out of the way for easier cleaning.
3. Mop as closely as possible around nonmovable equipment, making sure that strokes overlap and all areas get dusted.
4. Frequently shake out the mop into small piles to be picked up later; use a dustpan and handbrush to pick up piles.
5. Clean dust mop with a stiff brush; if quite soiled, have it laundered. Hang up mop to air.
6. Dust mopping is not recommended for kitchens; may be used in dining rooms and reception areas.

Wet-Mopping

Before wet-mopping, broom-sweep or dust-mop first. Move easily movable equipment and furniture out of the way.
Utensils and materials needed:

Broom or dust mop
Dust pan and hand brush
Putty knife
Two buckets, one with a wringer
Two mops, one for cleaning and one for rinsing and drying
Cleaning ingredient (should not damage floor)

Procedure

1. Prepare the cleaning solution. FOLLOW INSTRUCTIONS EX-ACTLY AS TO THE KIND OF CLEANER AND DILUTION.
2. Broom-sweep or dust-mop the area first (see instructions above).
3. Start mopping at the rear of floor to be washed, working backward and parallel to the wall. Clean a small area (approximately 10 × 10 feet) at one time. Mop corners by hand or use the heel of the mop.

4. Rinse the cleaned section with a rinse mop; rinse the mop, wring it out, and use it to dry the cleaned and rinsed area.
5. Repeat the wash-rinse-dry operation, until the entire floor is clean. CAUTION: Do not allow rinse water to get dirty; change it frequently.
6. Clean the dust mop or broom, buckets, handbrush, dustpan, and putty knife. Clean the mop in heavy-duty detergent or cleaner-sanitizer, rinse, and hang it up to dry.

Scrubbing (Hand or Machine)

Before scrubbing, dust-mop the floor first. Move easily movable equipment out of the way. (See directions for dust-mopping.)
Equipment, utensils, and materials needed:

Dust mop, dustpan, hand brush, putty knife
Two wet mops, one for applying cleaning solution and one for rinsing and drying
Scrub brushes for scrubbing by hand, or automatic scrubbing equipment
Two buckets, one for the cleaning solution and one for rinse water

Procedure

1. Prepare the cleaning solution. FOLLOW INSTRUCTIONS EXACTLY AS TO THE KIND OF CLEANER AND DILUTION.
2. Dust-mop the area first (see instructions above).
3. Wet-mop small sections (approximately 10′ × 10′) at one time.
4. Scrub by hand or machine.
5. Rinse each area twice; dry.
6. Always scrub corners and the strip along the baseboard and the baseboards by hand; clean up spatters on baseboards. CAUTION: Change wash and rinse water frequently.
7. Continue cleaner application-scrub-double rinse-dry sequence until the floor is done.
8. Clean mechanical equipment following the directions of the manufacturer. CAUTION: Never rest the scrubbing machine on the brushes, since it flattens and ruins them. Clean the mops, handbrushes, dustpan, and putty knife. Clean the buckets. Hang the wet mop and brushes to dry.

Care of Walls

All walls must be dusted as part of routine cleaning. Walls that become heavily soiled must also be washed. The frequency of washing walls must be judged by those responsible for scheduling cleaning. Walls that are spattered daily must be cleaned daily; walls that stay clean for weeks need occasional cleaning. No hard-and-fast rule is possible except that *walls must be kept clean and free of dust, moisture, grease, grime, and mildew.* Mildew can be a real problem in areas where moisture is high.

To be cleanable, walls and ceilings should be smooth and without cracks and crevices. Walls and ceilings should be vermin proof. Light-color walls make dirt more visible. Painted walls should be repainted regularly. Papered walls should be kept in a good state of upkeep, since loose paper offers hiding places for vermin.

How to Wash Walls and Woodwork

1. Dust painted walls before washing them, using, preferably, a vacuum cleaner; when dusting by broom or brush, dust is apt to be spread about. If a broom or brush must be used, cover it with a clean cloth. To remove cobwebs, use a lifting motion, because they are apt to be sticky and could cause streaks on wall if brushed downward.
2. Wash walls and woodwork with a cleaner that will not damage the surface.

Tile Walls

Utensils and materials needed:

Two buckets, one for washing and one for rinsing
Soft scrub brush
Sponges, cloths
Nonabrasive* cleansing powder (should not damage the tile)
Neutral detergent or other cleaner

Procedure

1. Wash the tiles with a sponge or cloth dipped in a warm, mild cleaning solution. Use a soft brush to clean between the tiles. If the walls have become grimy, a *non*abrasive cleansing powder may be used. However, frequent use of cleansing powder is damaging to tiles. Work from the bottom up to prevent streaking.
2. Clean a small area at one time, then rinse.
3. Rinse with clean warm water; change the rinse water frequently.
4. Dry with a soft, dry cloth.
5. Repeat the sequence wash-rinse-dry until the entire wall is clean.

* Nonabrasive means nonscratchy.

Painted Walls and Woodwork

General warning:

1. Painted surfaces are much more delicate than tile. *Do not use abrasives. Use a mild detergent or cleaner,* in proper dilution. READ THE LABEL ON THE PRODUCT. FOLLOW DIRECTIONS.
2. Rinse after using the cleaner, even if the directions on the label of the cleaner should state that rinsing may be omitted. Rinsing reduces the possibility of damage to paint.

Utensils and supplies needed:

Two buckets
Sponges, cloths
Warm solution of neutral detergent or mild soap
Warm water for rinsing sponges and cloths

1. Wash painted surfaces with a sponge dipped in cleaning solution. Work from the bottom up to avoid streaking. Streaks may form when the cleaning solution runs down on the soiled portion and dries there. Use cleaning solution on a small area at a time, then rinse and dry. Repeat the process until the entire surface is done.
2. Rinse. Wipe with a damp sponge or a cloth wrung out in clean warm water. *Caution:* Change the rinse water frequently.
3. Dry with a soft dry cloth.

Wallpaper (Washable)

1. Test the paper to ascertain whether the cleaner avoids roughing the surface, making the colors blend, or loosening the paper from the wall.
2. Follow the procedure for painted walls, but *never rub dry;* rather, gently pat dry. *Caution:* Great care is needed to avoid ruining the surface. Work very gently. Use as little water as possible. DO NOT RUB. The method described for nonwashable paper can be used for sensitive washable paper.

Wallpaper (Nonwashable)

1. Use wallpaper cleaner that looks like a lump of dough.
2. FOLLOW DIRECTIONS EXACTLY. The product is stroked over the paper, and dust particles and greasy soil should adhere to it. CAUTION: Knead the "dough" frequently to bring out clean surfaces; do not allow old soil to be spread back onto the paper.

Hood and Hood Filter

Hoods over stoves and fryers collect moist, greasy air. Hoods may become a sanitary hazard if they are not kept clean, because the drip from the hood may fall onto food and contaminate it. Hood filters do not function properly if they are gummed up with grease. Greasy hoods are also liable to cause fires, and are therefore dangerous from a safety point of view.

Filter. Wash the hood filter in the automatic dishwasher. Do this at least once a week, and daily if fryers and broilers are used daily.

Hood. Wash the hood, using the procedure described for walls. Use a detergent solution to remove grime. Rinse and dry. *Warning:* Be sure to use plenty of "elbow grease" to remove sticky accumulations from the channels each time the hood is washed.

How to Clean Washbowls, Toilet Bowls, and Urinals

Washbowls. The surface of washbowls may be scratched easily if abrasives are used. If soap scum has built up, a nonabrasive cleansing powder or a water softener such as Calgon may be used.

For regular care, washbowls should be cleaned simply with a solution of detergent and warm water.

Utensils and materials needed:

Detergent or other mild cleaner
Sponge
Cloth

Procedure

1. Rinse the basin by running the water for several seconds.
2. Wash out the basin with a sponge and detergent solution; remove built-up scum or stains with a nonabrasive cleaner or Calgon solution.
3. Rinse with clear water.
4. Dry with a soft cloth.
5. Wipe the chrome fixtures clean.

Toilet Bowls and Urinals. Toilet bowls and urinals are more resistant to chemical cleaners than are washbowls; therefore, certain chemicals can safely be used to clean them. *Use cleaners especially designed for toilets and urinals.* Toilet bowls and urinals should also be sanitized. FOLLOW DIRECTIONS EXACTLY. *Caution:* Never use toilet bowl and urinal cleaners on washbowls, since they may permanently damage the washbowls and render them difficult to keep sanitary.

Utensils and materials needed:

Special cleaner and sanitizer (detergent, disinfectant concentrate)
Special brushes
Cloths

Procedure

1. Flush commodes or urinals.
2. Pour the bowl cleaner into the bowls; if the bowls are stained, allow the cleaner to act for a while.
3. Using a bowl brush or mop, clean the entire bowl thoroughly and flush.
4. Using special applicators, apply disinfectant-cleaner solution to the bowl or urinal, inside and out.
5. Using a special applicator, wipe the tops and bottoms of toilet seats with a disinfectant-cleaner solution and wipe them dry with a cloth.

Windows, Mirrors and Lights

Frequent cleaning prevents build-up of greasy film; set up cleaning schedule to prevent this from happening.
Equipment and materials needed:

For daily routine vacuum-dusting or cleaning with water and a damp cloth, paper toweling or chamois is satisfactory.

Procedure

1. Use a sponge, chamois, or soft cloth; moisten it with water or cleaning solution; wring dry.
2. Wash the soiled surfaces.
3. Wipe with a dry, lint-free cloth, or a damp sponge, or a squeegee. When using a squeegee, stroke from the top to the bottom and wipe the squeegee after each stroke.

DO NOT WASH LIGHT FIXTURES WHILE THEY ARE STILL CONNECTED TO THE ELECTRIC OUTLET. Remove tubes and bulbs and clean with the window-washing solution.

Clean Equipment and Utensils

As stated by Fischback, a sanitation consultant: ". . . a clean wholesome meal is guaranteed the customer when you offer the menu. That is the responsibility of a food service operator. The food must be palatable, prepared by clean people, in clean utensils, with clean equipment. It should be served on clean dishes with clean tableware from a clean table on a clean floor, in clean surroundings."

A food-service operator can no longer fulfill his responsibility to the customer by providing quality food and service. He must also provide quality sanitation. Therefore, food-service managers and employees are really custodians of the health and welfare of their customers.

The primary objective of a cleaning operation in a public eating establishment is the control of bacteria. This is necessary (1) to prevent food spoilage, (2) to reduce health hazards, and (3) to control odors.

All food-preparation equipment and utensils may be contaminated with bacteria capable of producing disease and, therefore, this equipment constitutes a potential public-health hazard. Thorough cleaning and proper sanitizing are essential. Cleaning involves removing the soil, but sanitizing involves reducing the bacterial count to a safe level.

Fundamentally, the main cleaning agent is water. The use of cleaning compounds and friction helps water to do a better job. Cleaning is a practical application of chemistry. Since chemistry is one of the few exact sciences, successful cleaning involves the use of the proper amounts of detergent in clean water at the proper temperatures (110 to 120°F for handwashing and 130 to 140°F for machine washing).

The purpose of the detergent is to loosen the soil. Friction must be used to remove it. Friction is accomplished by cleaning tools (brushes and elbow grease) or cutting action by water sprays. Then the soil must be rinsed off or it will dry back onto the equipment surface. A clean surface is necessary for sanitizing because soil can inactivate the sanitizer. Clean water, at 170°F for 1 minute or at 180°F for 15 seconds, is necessary to rinse away soil and sanitize the equipment. If water at these temperatures is not available for the final rinse, then an approved sanitizer in proper strength (hypochlorites, 100 ppm, or quaternary compounds, 200 ppm) should be provided. Finally, any object that has been cleaned and sanitized must be placed on a clean surface and allowed to air-dry.

Before cleaning a specific type of equipment (utensil or surface) consideration must be given to the following factors.

1. *The nature of the water being used.* The water should be properly conditioned to make the detergent more effective and to eliminate the deposit of any minerals present in the water.

2. *The type of soil to be removed.* Soil may be grease, protein, mineral, or carbon. Thus, different types of cleaning compounds or different water temperatures may be required.

3. *The corrosion resistance of the material being cleaned.* This will determine the type and amount of friction that can be applied.

4. *The type of cleaner being employed.* Soap may leave a greasy film because of poor rinsing qualities; therefore, it is not recommended for general use. An abrasive may roughen the surface and increase the possibility of future soil. Most detergents, on the other hand, will do a good job if they are properly formulated and applied.

5. *The condition of the soil.* Soil may be fresh, soft, dried, or baked-on. Temperature plays an important role because soil that dries on at a low temperature is usually easy to remove, while baked-on residues create a highly specialized cleaning problem.

Proper sanitation of equipment begins at the time of purchase. The equipment should be designed for easy cleaning. Movable parts (particularly, those that come into contact with food) should be removed easily without the need of special tools. The remaining shell should be made of smooth, noncorrosive, nonchip material, free from screw heads, square corners, or cracks in which soil, grease, or food particles can lodge. It is as important to check the cleanability and the time required for cleaning a piece of equipment before purchase as it is to check the quality and capacity of production. If the equipment carries the National Sanitation Seal of Approval, the manager can be sure that it has met the requirements for cleanability; however, the time required for cleaning must be determined by test, preferably under actual operating conditions.

Proper installation is another major requirement for equipment sanitation. Stationary equipment should be installed far enough from the wall so the worker can clean behind it. Mobile models of most kitchen equipment are now available and should be considered for any new installations. Special attention must be given to water and utility line connections. A labyrinth of pipes or electrical cords creates a difficult cleaning problem and may constitute a safety hazard for the cleaner.

Good sanitation techniques in a food operation do not just happen. They result from a well-planned program that requires (1) the basic knowledge of what is involved in safe food handling, (2) the ability to translate this knowledge into practical and workable procedures to be followed in the daily routine of serving food that will ensure a wholesome product, and (3) a constant effort on the part of management not only to maintain the standards that have been set but also to emphasize their importance.

Food-service equipment can be classified under four major categories, listed below, and each category has its own sanitation significance.

1. *Equipment that comes into actual physical contact with the food material being processed.* This category includes all cutting, dicing, slicing, grinding, and mixing equipment, and all utensils, dishware, and chopping boards. Because of the physical contact between food and equipment, the possibility of microbial contamination is high; therefore, it is extremely important to use equipment that can be dismantled easily so contact parts can be taken to the scullery or the dishwasher for proper cleaning and sanitizing.

2. *Primary equipment used in cooking or holding food.* Ovens, ranges, broilers, and fryers are examples. Here the food does not come into actual contact with the equipment or, if it does, the contact is at temperatures that make the problem of microbial contamination negligible. The sanitation concern, then, becomes one of odor control, aesthetics, and equipment efficiency.

Soiled equipment is always a potential source of undesirable odor; where heat is involved, these odors are accentuated. The acrid odor emanating from a soiled deep-fat fryer has earned many a food-service operation the title of "The Greasy Spoon." Soiled equipment rarely works at optimum efficiency. A layer of burnt-on food on the oven hearth acts as an insulator and reduces oven temperature. It is poor economy to buy an oven with good thermostatic controls and then allow soil to destroy its efficiency. Proper maintenance of equipment not only controls odor but also cuts down on repair bills and extends the life of the equipment.

3. *Equipment used in cleaning other equipment.* Dishwashers and pot-and-pan sinks are common examples of this category of equipment. The importance of cleanliness should be obvious but, all too frequently, the proper cleaning of these machines is neglected because of an assumption that the large amounts of water and detergent used in the normal course of operation make these machines self-cleaning. Remember that dishes or utensils cannot be any cleaner than the machine in which they are washed.

Mineral deposits (which result from improperly conditioned water) and scrap trays filled with food residue provide excellent breeding spots for microorganisms. Scrap trays need to be emptied and washed after each meal, and mineral deposits should be removed regularly. Partially plugged wash-or-rinse arms in the machines destroy the uniform wash-and-rinse pattern necessary to produce clean dishes. They should be inspected daily and removed for cleaning when necessary.

Effective manual pot-and-pan washing requires a three-compartment sink with double drainboards. One drainboard provides a stacking surface for soiled pots and pans, and one is used for the air-drying of clean utensils after the sanitizing procedure. A double-walled compartment with a drain that has its overflow rim at the normal water level of the sink (between the wash and rinse compartments) permits the "skimming" of suds or grease films from the surface of the rinse water. Since grease and suds float, the skimming device allows them to be flushed off. Thus the rinse remains free of suds and grease film throughout the cleaning process.

4. *Transportation and mobile storage equipment.* This category of equipment, like primary equipment, does not usually come in contact with food, but does come in contact with pans, utensils, and dishes that, in turn, come in contact with food. Mobile dish-storage equipment, such as lowerators and dish carts, need special attention. Dishes are only as clean as the equipment in which they are stored.

Management must keep in mind that equipment designed for easy cleaning will be clean only to the degree of cleanliness demanded by management and exercised by the worker. The worker, in addition to being provided the necessary tools and cleaning compounds, must be trained to do the job properly. A demonstration by the manager or the supervisor of how the job should be done, followed by a practice period under supervision, will assure management that the worker has learned to do the job correctly. A written cleaning procedure is a useful training tool and serves as a standard for checking the quality of performance. Daily inspection by management of all routine cleaning is extremely important to the success of the program.

A checklist of all items that are to be cleaned should be developed. Since it is safe to assume that all equipment in the kitchen needs to be cleaned at some time, a systematic method of listing the equipment should be used. The operator should start at one end of the kitchen and move to the other end, listing all equipment and grouping like equipment together. This will eliminate the possibility of overlooking some of the items. The second step is to determine how often each item on the list should be cleaned. The third step is to develop a cleaning schedule in such a manner that all items on the checklist are delegated to a definite person at a definite time. These cleaning assignments should then be incorporated into the employee work schedules. Written cleaning schedules and cleaning procedures are the tools that management uses to control the sanitation program. The cleaning schedule determines who is responsible for the job, and the cleaning procedure prescribes how the work is to be accomplished. Daily follow-up is a "must" for an effective sanitation program. The format of all cleaning procedures should:

1. Give the name of the equipment being cleaned.
2. Have three columns headed "when," "how," and "use."
3. Include all steps (written as briefly as possible) that are necessary to properly dismantle, clean, and reassemble the equipment.
4. Take into consideration the safety precautions necessary to make the equipment safe to clean.
5. Specify the amount of detergent to use and the temperature of water to use for washing, rinsing and sanitizing.
6. Stress the need for a clean surface for air drying and clean hands for reassembling equipment.
7. Provide a separate procedure if daily cleaning differs from weekly or bimonthly cleaning.

The following cleaning procedures are offered as examples of the type that can serve both as a training tool and a standard for evaluating the effectiveness of performance. These procedures are based on a specific model of each type of equipment. Remember that there are many different models available. Therefore, the dismantling and reassembling instructions may need to be changed to conform to the specific model in use in any given food service.

The proper proportion of detergent to water required for each cleaning job should be specified. Because of the variety of detergents available, it has not been possible to specify the amounts of detergents to be used in these generalized procedures. Each operator must determine the appropriate amount of detergent available in his operation for each cleaning job. Employees should be provided with convenient measuring and weighing equipment so the correct amount of detergent will be used. If more than one type of cleaning material is available, the name of the correct cleaning material and the amount to be used should be part of the cleaning procedure.

Procedure 1.   How to Clean Food Slicer

When	How	Use
After each use	1. Turn off machine	
	2. Remove electric cord from socket	
	3. Set blade control to zero	
	4. Remove meat carriage (a) Turn knob at bottom of carriage	
	5. Remove the back blade guard (a) Loosen knob on the guard	
	6. Remove the top blade guard (a) Loosen knob at center of blade	
	7. Take parts to pot-and-pan sink, scrub	Hot machine detergent solution, gong brush
	8. Rinse	Clean hot water, 170°F for 1 minute. Use double S hook to remove parts from hot water
	9. Allow parts to air dry on clean surface	
	10. Wash blade and machine shell CAUTION: PROCEED WITH CARE WHILE BLADE IS EXPOSED	Use damp bunched cloth[a] dipped in hot machine detergent solution
	11. Rinse	Clean hot water, clean bunched cloth
	12. Sanitize blade, allow to air dry	Clean water, chemical sanitizer, clean bunched cloth
	13. Replace front blade guard immediately after cleaning shell (a) Tighten knob	
	14. Replace back blade guard (a) Tighten knob	
	15. Replace meat carriage (a) Tighten knob	
	16. Leave blade control at zero	
	17. Replace electric cord into socket	

[a] Fold cloth to several thicknesses.

Procedure 2.   How to Clean Vegetable Chopper

When	How	Use
After each use	1. Turn off switch, wait until blades have stopped	
	2. Release safety lock[a]	
	3. Turn cover lock one fourth turn and pull up	
	4. Raise cover to upright position	
	5. Remove blade guide	
	(a) Lift up	
	(b) Place in bowl	
	6. Remove blade	
	(a) Remove knob on blade shaft	
	(b) Grasp blade at the dull surfaces near the shaft	
	(c) Pull blade off shaft	
	(d) Place blade into bowl	
	CAUTION: HANDLE BLADE WITH CARE	
	7. Lift off cover	
	8. Remove bowl	
	(a) Give bowl one half turn clockwise and lift	
	9. Take cover, bowl, blade guide, and blade to sink and scrub	Hot machine detergent solution, gong brush
	CAUTION: NEVER PLACE BLADE IN SINK; LEAVE ON DRAINBOARD UNTIL READY FOR WASHING AND RINSING	
	10. Rinse parts, allow to air dry on clean surface	Clean hot water, 170°F for 1 minute
	11. Scrub shell of machine	Clean damp cloth dipped into hot machine detergent solution
	12. Rinse shell, wipe dry	Clean hot water, clean dry cloth
	13. Reassemble chopper	
	(a) Replace bowl, place on spindle, give half turn counterclockwise	
	(b) Replace cover, leave in upright position	
	(c) Replace blade guide and blade	
	(d) Close cover, put on safety lock	

[a] In new models, safety lock is part of switch.

Procedure 3. How to Clean Vertical Cutter/Mixer

When	How	Use

After each use	1. Turn cutter motor to "off" position
	   (a) Open inspection cover on top
	   (b) Wait until blades have stopped
	2. Release cover lock
	3. Raise cover
	4. Fill bowl half full of hot machine detergent solution
	5. Close and lock cover
	   (a) Close inspection cover
	6. Turn cutter motor to "on" position Allow to run 30 seconds
	7. Turn cutter motor to "off" position
	   (a) Open inspection cover
	   (b) Wait until blades have stopped
	8. Release cover lock
	9. Raise cover
	10. Tilt bowl to remove water
	   (a) Remove locking pin at base of bowl
	   (b) Release lever to tilt kettle
	   (c) Lock lever to hold bowl in new position
	11. Rinse inside and outside of bowl, cover, and frame
	12. Wipe outside of machine, frame, and cover until dry; allow inside to air dry
	13. Return bowl to upright position
	   (a) Remove locking pin
	   (b) Release lever to raise bowl
	   (c) Lock lever to help hold bowl
	14. Close cover, do not lock
	   (a) Leave inspection cover open
		Hot water, detergent
		
		Large pail or floor drain
		
		Hose, hot water
		
		Clean dry cloth

Daily	1. Turn cutter motor to "off" position
	   (a) Open inspection cover on top
	   (b) Wait until blades have stopped
	2. Remove mixing baffle
	   (a) Loosen nut on top of cover and withdraw handle
	   (b) Release cover lock
	   (c) Raise cover to upright position
	   (d) Withdraw mixing baffle and shaft	

When	How	Use
	3. Remove plastic inspection cover and gasket	
	4. Remove blade shaft (a) Turn blade shaft lock clockwise to remove (b) Pull up on blade shaft	
	5. Take parts to sink and scrub CAUTION: LEAVE BLADESHAFT ON DRAINBOARD UNTIL READY FOR WASHING AND RINSING	Hot machine detergent solution, gong brush
	6. Rinse parts and allow to air dry on clean surface	Clean hot water, 170°F for 1 minute
	7. Fill bowl half full of hot machine detergent solution	Hot water and detergent
	8. Scrub bowl, motor stem, and inside and outside of cover; scrub side of bowl and frame	Gong brush
	9. Tilt bowl to remove water (a) Remove locking pin at base of bowl (b) Release lever to tilt kettle (c) Tighten lever with bowl in new position (d) Replace locking pin to hold position	Large pail or floor drain
	10. Rinse inside and outside of bowl, cover, and frame; wipe outside, allow inside to air dry	Hose, hot water, clean dry cloth
	11. Return bowl to upright position (a) Remove locking pin at base of bowl (b) Release lever to raise bowl (c) Lock lever to help hold bowl (d) Replace locking pin	
	12. Reassemble parts (a) Replace blade shaft, lock in position (screw on tight) (b) Replace gasket (c) Replace mixing baffle and shaft into cover (d) Close cover (e) Replace plastic inspection cover (f) Replace handle	

When	*How*	*Use*
	(g) Replace nut on top of cover, tighten	
	13. Leave cover closed, do not lock	
	(a) Partially open inspection cover	

Figure 18. Vertical vegetable cutter. (Courtesy of Hobart Mfg. Co.)

Procedure 4.   How to Clean Food Mixer

When	How	Use
After each use	1. Turn off machine	
	2. Remove bowl and beaters, take to pot-and-pan sink for cleaning	Hot machine detergent solution, short handled gong brush
	3. Rinse, keep immersed for 1 minute, air dry	Clean hot running water 170°-180°F
Daily	4. Scrub machine (a) Beater shaft (b) Bowl saddle (c) Shell and base	Hot machine detergent solution, gong brush, clean cloth
	5. Rinse	Clean damp cloth wrung out in clean hot water
	6. Dry	Clean dry cloth
	7. Oil as per directions if required	Machine oil

Procedure 5.   How to Clean Steak Machine

When	How	Use
After each use	1. Turn off machine	
	2. Remove electric cord from socket	
	3. Remove guard	
	4. Remove cutter roll assembly (a) Loosen locks (b) Pull entire roll assembly to right to remove from machine	
	5. Take guard and cutter roll assembly to sink (a) Remove handle (b) Remove blade guides, handle cutter roll with care	Pot-and-pan sink or sink in meat shop
	(c) Clean excess meat particles from cutter roll	Special cleaning fork
	CAUTION: PLACE CUTTER ROLL ON DRAINBOARD UNTIL READY FOR WASHING	
	6. Scrub all parts	Hot machine detergent solution, stiff brush
	7. Put all parts into wire basket and immerse in rinse	Clean, hot water, 170°F for 1 minute
	8. Allow to air dry in basket on clean surface	
	9. Clean shell of machine	Clean damp cloth, dipped in hot detergent solution
	10. Rinse	Clean, hot water, cloth

When	How	Use
	11. Dry shell	Clean dry cloth
	12. Reassemble cutter roll:	
	(a) Replace blade guides	
	(b) Replace handles	
	(c) Replace roll assembly into socket	
	(d) Lock roll assembly	
	(e) Replace guard	
	13. Replace electric cord into socket	

Procedure 6. How to Clean Power Meat Saw

When	How	Use
After each use	1. Turn off power	
	2. Remove parts:	
	(a) *Pan.* Open bottom door to remove pan	
	(b) *Small table section.* Tilt and slide gauge plate to the back. Lift out small table section	
	(c) *Blade.* Turn blade control clockwise to loosen tension. Pull back guard down to swing free of blade. Coil blade	
	(d) *Meat scrapers.* Release spring clip and slide from shaft	
	(e) *Blade wheels (upper and lower).* Loosen knob and remove	
	(f) *Moving table.* Release safety catch below table and slide off	
	(g) *Lower blade roller.* Release thumb screw in front at base and remove	
	(h) *Blade guide.* Remove setscrew on top and pull down to release; replace setscrew while washing blade guide	
	3. Take all parts to sink for washing	Hot machine detergent solution, gong brush and small vegetable brush
	4. Rinse:	
	(a) Place small parts in wire basket and immerse	Clean hot water, 170°F Long-handled wire basket
	(b) Immerse large parts	
	(c) Leave all parts immersed at least one minute	

When	How	Use
	(d) Remove parts to clean surface; allow to air dry	Wire basket and double S hook
	5. Clean machine shell	
	(a) Remove all meat particles	Hand
	(b) Scrub down machine	Hot machine detergent solution, clean cloth and brush
	6. Rinse	Clean hot water
	7. Wipe dry	Clean dry cloth
	8. Replace parts in reverse order	

Procedure 7. How to Clean Food Grinder

When	How	Use
After each use	1. Turn off machine	
	2. Remove electric cord from socket	
	3. Loosen ring on grinder, release safety clamp	
	4. Remove pan and grinder head and take to pot-and-pan sink	
	(a) Remove ring	Ice pick and/or stiff brush, hand
	(b) Take out plate, remove food particles	
	(c) Remove knife	
	(d) Remove feed screw from cylinder	
	5. Wash parts in pot-and-pan sink, give special attention to threads and grooves in cylinder and ring	Hot machine detergent solution, gong brush, ice pick
	CAUTION: DO NOT PUT KNIFE INTO SINK; LEAVE ON DRAINBOARD UNTIL READY FOR WASHING	
	6. Put all clean parts in wire basket and immerse in rinse	Clean hot water, 170°F for 1 minute
	7. Remove to clean dry surface and allow to air dry	
	8. Oil threads on ring and cylinder	Salad oil
	9. Clean outside of grinder shell	Hot machine detergent solution, clean cloth
	10. Rinse shell	Clean hot water, cloth
	11. Wipe dry	Clean dry cloth
	12. Store grinder parts in appropriate place[a]	

[a] Do not reassemble unless the next job requires same size plate.

Procedure 8. How to Clean Bench Can Opener

When	How	Use
Daily	1. Remove shank to pot-and-pan sink	
	2. Scrub, give special attention to blade and moving parts	Hot machine detergent solution, gong brush
	3. Rinse	Clean hot water, 170°F for 1 minute
	4. Allow to air dry on clean surface	
	5. Inspect blade and replace when notched	
	6. Scrub base plate attached to table	Hot machine detergent solution, gong brush
	7. Rinse base plate	Clean hot water, cloth
	8. Replace shank	
Periodically	1. Remove base plate from table	Screw driver
	(a) Scrape area free of all food particles	Putty knife
	(b) Scrub area	Hot machine detergent solution, gong brush
	(c) Rinse	Clean hot water, cloth
	(d) Replace base plate	Screw driver

Procedure 9. How to Clean Platform Scales

When	How	Use
Daily	1. Remove weights	To cart or table
	2. Scrub platform	Hot machine detergent solution, gong brush
	3. Rinse	Clean hot water, cloth
	4. Wipe dry	Clean dry cloth
	5. Replace weights	
Weekly	1. Remove weights	To cart or tables
	2. Scrub platform, frame, weights, and wheels (tip scale to side to clean wheels)	Hot machine detergent solution, gong brush, clean cloth
	3. Rinse	Clean hot water, cloth
	4. Wipe dry	Clean dry cloth
	5. Replace weights	

Procedure 10. How to Clean Table Scales (Even Balance)

When	How	Use
After each use	1. Remove scale pan	
	2. Brush all dry particles from scale frame and surrounding table top	Clean dry cloth
	3. Wash scales, scale pan, and table top beneath and surrounding scales	Hot machine detergent solution, gong brush, clean cloth
	4. Rinse and sanitize scale pan[a]	Clean hot water, chemical sanitizer
	5. Allow scale pan to air dry Wipe scale frame dry	Clean dry cloth

[a] Scale pan can be washed in pot sink and sanitized with 170°F water for 1 minute.

Procedure 11. How to Clean Portion-Control Scales

When	How	Use
After each use	1. Brush off any food particles on platform	Clean damp cloth
	2. Scrub platform and frame; give special attention to notched balance beam	Hot machine detergent solution, gong brush, clean cloth
	3. Rinse and sanitize platform, allow platform to air dry	Clean hot water, chemical sanitizer, clean cloth
	4. Wipe scale frame dry	Clean dry cloth
	5. Set scale on clean surface	
	6. Scrub table top	Hot machine detergent solution, gong brush, clean cloth
	7. Rinse table top and wipe dry	Clean hot water, clean dry cloth
	8. Return scales to proper position	

Procedure 12. How to Clean Chopping Boards

When	How	Use
After each use	1. Take chopping board to pot and pan sink	
	2. Scrub immediately or place on soiled pan drainboard	Hot machine detergent solution, gong brush
	CAUTION: DO NOT SOAK CHOPPING BOARD	
	3. Rinse	Clean hot running water
	4. Sanitize	Clean hot water, chemical sanitizer
	5. Prop on end and allow to air dry	Clean dry surface

Procedure 13.   How to Clean Pots, Pans, and Small Utensils (Manual)

When	How	Use
After each use	1. Place soiled pots and pans on left-hand drainboard (a) Place small utensils in one pot	
	2. Fill soak sink ¾ full	Hot water, approximately 120°F
	3. Scrape food particles from pots and pans	Heavy spatula, garbage disposal

	4. Place pans into soak sink
	   (a) Place small utensils in one pot; avoid bending or crushing beaters and wire whips
	   CAUTION: DO NOT PLACE KNIVES OR SHARP UTENSILS IN SINK; WASH AND RINSE IMMEDIATELY AND ALLOW TO AIR DRY ON CLEAN DRAINBOARD
	   (b) Allow pans to soak while preparing other 2 sinks	

	5. Measure detergent into wash sink; fill ¾ full	Detergent Hot water, approximately 120°F
	6. Fill rinse sink ¾ full	Hot running water, 170°F or above[a]
	7. Scrub pots and pans in soak sink; transfer to wash sink	Metal sponge, gong brush

	8. Scrub pots and pans
	   (a) Transfer clean pots and pans to rinse sink, open side up
	   (b) Do not allow pots and pans to nest
	   (c) Place small utensils in one pot to avoid damage and make removal easier
		Hot detergent solution

	9. Allow pans to remain immersed for one minute	Hot running water, 170°F or above
	10. Remove pots and pans, place open side down, and allow to air dry (a) Do not allow pans to nest	Double S Hook Clean drainboard
	11. Stack dry pans in appropriate	

[a] Hot water booster tank or steam line in rinse sink may be required to maintain 170°F. If this temperature cannot be maintained, pots and pans will need to be sanitized with a chemical sanitizer.

When	How	Use
	place on clean pot and pan rack open side down	
	12. Return small utensils to appropriate drawer or hang on utensil rack	
	13. Change soak and wash water as often as necessary	Follow steps 2 and 5

Procedure 14.   How to Clean Pots, Pans, and Small Utensils (Machine)

When	How	Use
After each use	1. Follow steps 1 through 4 on manual procedure	
	2. Fill pot and pan machine	Hot water
	(a) Open steam valve or turn on gas burner	
	3. Fill detergent dispenser	Detergent
	4. Rack pots and pans	Appropriate rack
	(a) Put like pans together	
	(b) Do not overload or allow pans to nest	
	5. Push start button	
	6. Push rack into machine	Automatic wash-and-rinse cycle
	7. Remove rack from machine	
	8. Allow pans to air dry	Clean drainboard
	(a) Do not allow pans to nest	
	9. Stack dry pans on clean pot and pan rack, open side down	
	10. Return small utensils to appropriate drawer or utensil rack	
	11. Change water in soak sink as often as necessary	
	12. Clean pot and pan machine as often as necessary	

Procedure 15.   How to Wash Dishes, Glassware and Flatware (Flite-Type Machine)[a]

When	How	Use
SOILED DISH STATION:		
After each use	1. Fill dish machine	Hot water
	2. Turn on steam	
	3. Fill detergent dispenser and rinse dry dispenser	
	4. Scrape, prerinse, and stack dishes according to size and type	Prerinse unit, garbage disposal
	5. Rack cups and glasses open side down	Cup and glass racks
	6. Separate flatware according to type	
	7. Place flatware into perforated baskets with business side up; soak	Perforated flatware baskets Flatware soaking sink
	8. Check temperature on wash-and-rinse tank	Prerinse 120°F Wash 130° to 140°F Rinse 170° to 185°F
	9. Push start button on machine	
	10. Place glass racks on conveyor belt	Automatic wash and rinse
	11. Place cup racks on conveyor belt	
	12. Rack dishes on belt according to size and type	
	13. Place filled flatware baskets in cup rack (a) Place rack on conveyor belt	
CLEAN DISH STATION:		
	14. Inspect glasses for cleanliness (set aside soiled glassware and return to soiled-dish table)	
	15. Remove glass racks from belt	To a clean dolly
	16. Inspect cups for cleanliness; remove any soiled cups.	
	17. Remove cup rack from belt	To a clean dolly
	18. Remove dishes from belt, inspect for cleanliness, and stack according to size and type	Clean dish table or appropriate dish cart
	19. Remove flatware (a) Inspect for cleanliness	
	20. Transfer clean flatware to clean	Perforated flatware

[a] Dish washer should check water temperature, detergent, and rinse-dry dispensers frequently to be sure machine is being operated properly.

When	How	Use
	perforated basket, business side down	basket
	20. Send flatware through dish machine a second time	
	21. Remove flatware basket from belt	Clean dish table or appropriate flatware cart
	22. Transport dishes, glasses, and flatware to point of use	Cart

Procedure 16. How to Clean Rotary Toaster

When	How	Use
After each use	1. Brush crumbs from front surface of toaster behind bread racks	Small stiff-bristled brush
	2. Remove slanted toast guide and tray below toaster	
	3. Brush dry crumbs from guide, tray, under the toaster, and surrounding table top	Clean dry cloth
	4. Wash toaster frame and area under toaster	Clean damp cloth dipped into hot machine detergent solution
	5. Wash guide, tray, and surrounding table top	Same as above
	6. Rinse	Clean hot water, cloth
	7. Wipe dry	Clean dry cloth
	8. Replace toast guide and tray	

Procedure 17. How to Clean Automatic Toaster

When	How	Use
After each use	1. Remove electric plug from socket	
	2. Brush interior of each slot free of crumbs	Small stiff-bristled brush
	CAUTION: AVOID INJURY TO WIRES	
	3. Pull out crumb tray beneath toaster, brush free of crumbs	Clean dry cloth or soft brush
	4. Move toaster, brush crumbs from table top	Same as above
	5. Wash table top, toaster, and crumb tray	Clean damp cloth dipped in hot machine detergent solution
	6. Rinse	Clean hot water, cloth

When	How	Use
	7. Wipe dry	Clean dry cloth
	8. Replace toaster and crumb tray	
	9. Connect electric plug to socket	

Procedure 18.   How to Clean Coffee Urn

When	How	Use
After each use	1. Lift cover	
	2. Remove bag or filter[a]	
	(a) Empty grounds	
	(b) Wash urn bag or filter	Hot running water
	(c) Soak bag when not in use	Cold water
	3. Drain urn	
	4. Close drain	
	5. Rinse urn and drain	Clean hot water, long-handled gong brush
	6. Close drain; remake coffee as needed	
Daily	1. Follow steps 1 through 5 above	
	2. Close drain and partially fill	Hot water
	3. Scrub urn and inside of cover	Long-handled gong brush
	4. Drain urn	
	5. Flush urn with faucet open	Hot water
	6. Clean glass gauge	
	(a) Remove nut at top of tube	
	(b) Insert brush and plunge up and down	Hot water, urn cleaner gauge brush
	(c) rinse gauge glass	Clean hot water, measuring cup with pouring lip
	7. Clean faucet and shank	
	(a) Remove faucet from shank	
	(b) Scrub inside of shank into urn	Hot water, urn cleaner
	(c) Scrub inside of faucet	Gauge brush
	(d) Rinse faucet	Clean hot water
	(e) Assemble faucet to shank	
	(f) Rinse shank; partially fill urn, leave faucet open	Clean hot water
	8. Close faucet	
	9. Partially fill urn with water, leave until the next service	2 gallons of water
	10. Wipe outside of urn and cover	Clean damp cloth
	Scrub drain and urn stand	Hot machine detergent

[a] Coffee grounds should be removed as soon as coffee is finished.

When	How	Use
	11. Wipe dry	Clean dry cloth
	12. Leave urn open	
Two to three times a week	1. Follow steps 1 to 5 in "after each use" schedule	
	2. Close drain	
	3. Partially fill urn with water and urn cleaner and mix well	Hot water, one package of urn cleaner, long-handled gong brush
	4. Allow solution to stand 30 to 45 minutes	
	5. Follow steps 3 to 12 in the "Daily" Schedule	

Procedure 19. How to Clean Potato Peeler

When	How	Use
After each use	1. Flush out machine while machine is running[a]	Clean cold water
	2. Turn off machine, allow disc to stop	
Daily	3. Remove lid	
	4. Lift abrasive disc by sunken handles	
	5. Flush machine again if any peelings remain	Clean cold water
	6. Scrub inside and outside of machine, give special attention to crevices around door	Hot water, gong brush
	7. Disassemble peel trap (a) Remove lid (b) Remove strainer (c) Remove stopper	
	8. Flush peel trap Scrub	Cold water Hot water, gong brush
	9. Take parts to sink and scrub (a) Lid (b) Disc (c) Strainer (d) Stopper	Hot water, gong brush[b]

[a] Always flush machine with cold water prior to using hot water. Hot water will cause peelings to cook onto metal and make cleaning more difficult.

[b] Do not use detergent on the abrasive disc; it is difficult to rinse off all the detergent.

When	How	Use
	10. Rinse parts and allow to air dry	Clean hot water
	11. Wipe exterior	Clean damp cloth
	12. Reassemble:	
	(a) Replace disc	
	(b) Replace stopper and strainer in peel trap	
	(c) Leave lid off peeler and peel trap to air	
	(d) Leave door open to air	

Procedure 20. How to Clean Steam-Jacketed Kettle

When	How	Use
After each use	1. Turn off steam, allow kettle to cool	
	2. Open drain	
	3. Flush kettle	Lukewarm water Long-handled gong brush
	4. Close drain, remove drain screen[a]	
	5. Fill kettle to cover highest food line, add detergent, mix well	Hot water, detergent Long-handled gong brush
	6. Withdraw approximately 2 quarts of water to charge outlet pipe	Gallon measure
	7. For cooked-on soil, allow solution to stand for 30 to 60 minutes	
	8. Scrub kettle, inside and out, scrub cover inside and out, scrub frame and drain cover	Hot machine detergent solution, long-handled gong brush
	9. Open drain, remove valve core shell and outlet port	
	10. Rinse kettle and all parts	Clean hot water
	11. Reassemble outlet port	
	12. Close drain	
	13. Sanitize outlet port, drain	Chemical sanitizer in proper solution
	14. Close drain, replace drain screen	
	15. Allow inside of kettle to air dry	
	16. Wipe outside of kettle, cover, and frame	Clean dry cloth
	17. Close cover	

[a] Newer models may not have drain covers.

Procedure 21.   How to Clean Stack Steamer

When	How	Use
Daily	1. Turn off steam, allow to cool	
	2. Start cleaning with top deck	
	3. Turn center wheel counterclockwise to open	
	4. Remove shelves[a] (a) Release safety catch under shelf (b) Lift shelf up and out	
	5. Take shelves to pot-and-pan sink	
	6. Scrub top and bottom of shelves	Hot machine detergent solution, gong brush
	7. Rinse	Clean hot water, 170°F for 1 minute
	8. Allow shelves to air dry on clean surface	
	9. Scrub chambers, check to see that all drains are open, scrub outside, sides, and top of steamer	Hot machine detergent solution, gong brush, gauge brush
	10. Rinse chambers, outside and top	Clean hot water, clean cloth
	11. Close steamer, turn on for 1 minute	
	12. Turn off steamer, open, allow to air dry	
	13. Replace shelves, fasten safety lock, test lock	
	14. Wipe off outside and top of steamer	Clean dry cloth
	15. Leave doors ajar	

[a] Newer models may have pan glide instead of shelves.

Procedure 22.   How to Clean Hi-Pressure Steamer

When	How	Use
Daily	1. Turn off steam	
	2. Allow to cool	
	3. Turn center wheel counterclockwise as far as it will go; push to right to open	
	4. Scrub inside and outside of chamber, give special attention to pan glides, clean drain	Hot machine detergent solution, gong brush, gauge brush
	5. Rinse chamber, inside and out	Clean hot water Clean cloth

When	How	Use
	6. Close door, turn on steam for 1 minute	
	7. Open door, allow to air dry	
	8. Wipe outside and top	Clean dry cloth

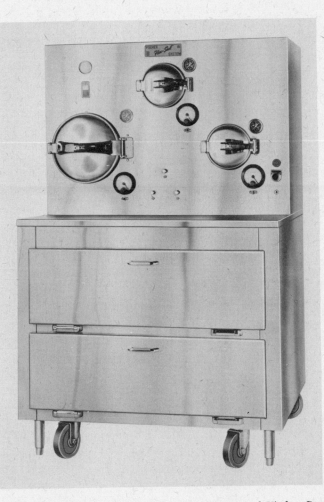

Figure 19. Hi-pressure steamer with freezer base. (Courtesy of Vischer Products Co.)

Procedure 23.   How to Clean Electric Overhead Broiler (Salamander)

When	How	Use
After each use	1. Turn off broiler, allow to cool	
	2. Remove grid:	
	(a) Pull lift lever to left	
	(b) Move grid to highest position	
	(c) Lift grid up and out	
	3. Take grid to pot-and-pan sink, soak	Hot machine detergent solution
	4. Scrape any burnt particles from sides of broiler	Long-handled scraper
	5. Remove grease tray, empty grease	Waste-fat container
	6. Take grease tray to pot-and-pan sink	
	7. Scrub broiler grid and grease tray	Hot machine detergent solution, gong brush
	8. Rinse grid and grease tray, allow to air dry on clean surface	Clean hot water, 170°F for 1 minute
	9. Wipe inside of broiler	Clean damp cloth wrung out in hot machine detergent solution
	CAUTION: DO NOT USE TOO MUCH WATER; DO NOT WASH CALROD UNITS— THEY ARE SELF-CLEANING	
	10. Wipe outside and top of broiler	Same as above
	11. Rinse inside, outside, and top of broiler, wipe dry	Clean damp cloth wrung out in clean hot water, clean dry cloth
	12. Replace grease tray	
	13. Replace grid	
	(a) Lock into position	
	(b) Test grid to see if it will roll out and lock	

Procedure 24.   How to Clean Gas Frialator

When	How	Use
After each use	1. Allow fat to cool but not solidify	
	2. Drain and strain fat[a]	Cheese cloth, 2 or 3 thicknesses, clean pot
	(a) Secure cheesecloth to pot to form strainer	
	(b) Place pot below drain	
	(c) Open drain	
	(d) Close drain after all fat has been removed	
	(e) Move fat from frialator	

[a] Or use commercial fat-filter machine, and pump filtered shortening into clean pot.

When	How	Use
	3. Fill frialator, scrub inside and outside of unit	Hot machine detergent solution, long-handled gong brush
	4. Place large pot below drain and open drain	Large pot
	5. Rinse frialator thoroughly	Clean hot water
	6. Wipe dry	Clean dry cloth
	7. Refill frialator[b]	Strained fat
	8. Cover when not in use	
Before changing to new fat	1. Allow fat to cool but not to solidify	
	2. Drain fat and dispose	Frozen fruit cans, 30#
	3. Flush unit thoroughly to remove all sediment	Hot water, waste container
	4. Fill frialator	Warm water, detergent, or deep-fry cleaner
	5. Turn on frialator and boil for 30 minutes[c]	
	6. While boiling, scrub inside of the frialator	Long-handled gong brush, rubber gloves
	CAUTION: AVOID SPLASHING ANY SOLUTION ON SKIN OR IN EYES. IF ANY COMES IN CONTACT WITH SKIN, FLUSH IMMEDIATELY WITH LARGE QUANTITIES OF CLEAR WATER[d]	
	7. Drain frialator	Waste container
	8. Rinse unit thoroughly	Hot water
	9. Refill tank	Warm water, detergent
	10. Brush all inside surfaces, give special attention to burners and crevices under burners, clean outside	Long-handled brush
	11. Drain	Waste container
	12. Rinse	Hot water, ½ cup white vinegar
	13. Dry thoroughly	Clean dry cloth
	14. Fill with new fat	
	15. Cover when not in use	

[b] If frialator is not used daily, grease clean frialator lightly with clean shortening, cover, and store strained shortening in refrigerator.

[c] Put burner grids from range into this solution and boil—see procedure on page 107.

[d] Protective eye goggles may be required by law.

Procedure 25.   How to Clean Electric Frialator

When	How	Use
After each use	1. Allow fat to cool but not solidify	
	2. Lift calrod unit from fat, lock into position	
	3. Turn on frialator to high temperature (calrod units are self-cleaning)[a]	
	4. Take clean container from storage cabinet below unit; place on range or cart next to frialator	Clean frialator container
	5. Pump fat from frialator through filter into clean container	Commercial fat filter machine
	6. Remove soiled container from frialator, take to pot-and-pan sink for cleaning	Hot machine detergent solution, gong brush
	7. Rinse and allow to air dry	Clean hot water, 170°F for 1 minute
	8. Turn off frialator, allow unit to cool	
	9. Scrub shell, surrounding frame and outside	Hot machine detergent solution, clean damp cloth
	10. Rinse and wipe dry	Clean hot water, clean dry cloth
	11. Lift clean container with strained fat into frialator[b]	
	12. Remove safety lock, lower calrod unit into fat	
	13. Cover when not in use	

[a] If time permits, clean calrod units first, then proceed with remainder of schedule.

[b] If frialator is not used daily, cover and store strained fat in refrigerator.

Procedure 26.   How to Clean Electric Fry Pan

When	How	Use
After each use	1. Turn off switch	
	2. Raise cover	
	3. Flush pan to remove all loose food particles	Lukewarm water, gong brush
	4. Tilt pan to remove water	Large pail or floor drain
	(a) Turn wheel at right side of	

When	How	Use
	pan counterclockwise to pouring position[a]	
	5. Return pan to upright position (a) Turn wheel clockwise	
	6. Fill fry pan to highest food line	Hot water, detergent
	7. Scrub pan, give special attention to cover and pouring lip; scrub outside of pan, cover, and frame	Gong brush
	8. Tilt pan to remove water (a) Turn wheel counterclockwise	Large pail or floor drain
	9. Rinse pan inside and out	Hose, hot water
	10. Return pan to upright position (a) Turn wheel clockwise	
	11. Allow inside to air dry; wipe outside of pan, cover, and frame dry	Clean dry cloth
	12. Close cover	

[a] Place bun pan in front of pouring lip to guide water to floor drain and to prevent splashing.

Figure 20.   Electric fry pan. (Courtesy of Groen Mfg. Co.)

Procedure 27.   How to Clean Ranges

When	How	Use
GRILL PLATES After each use	1. Allow plate to cool	
	2. Scrape grill to loosen burned-on particles	Heavy turner or putty knife
	3. Remove loose particles	Cloth, dust pan
	4. Scrub grill plate	Hot machine detergent solution, gong brush
	5. Scrub grease trough	Same as above
	6. Scrub back apron	Same as above
	7. Remove, dump, and wash grease trap	Same as above
	8. Rinse and wipe dry	Clean hot water Clean dry cloth
OPEN TOP Daily	1. Allow range to cool	
	2. Lift out burner grids, take to sink and scrub	Hot machine detergent solution, gong brush Wire brush
	3. Rinse, wipe dry	Clean hot water, clean dry cloth
	4. Brush burners, light burners to check for clogged burners	Wire brush, ice pick
	5. Clean back apron and warming oven	Hot machine detergent, clean damp cloth
	6. Remove grease and/or warming trays below burners; take to sink and scrub	Same as above
	7. Rinse and wipe dry	Clean hot water, clean dry cloth
	8. Replace clean grids and trays	
SOLID TOP Daily	1. Allow range to cool	
	2. Loosen all burned-on particles	Putty knife, dust pan
	3. Scrub top of range (keep water to minimum)	Hot machine detergent solution, gong brush, clean damp cloth
	4. Clean back apron and warming oven	Same as above
	5. Rinse and wipe dry	Clean hot water, clean dry cloth

When	How	Use
	6. Apply rust preventative to solid tops	Salad oil or clean shortening
OUTSIDE OF ALL RANGES Daily	1. Scrub fronts, sides, and back	Hot machine detergent solution, clean damp cloth
	2. Rinse	Clean hot water
	3. Wipe dry	Clean dry cloth
	4. Polish all metal trim	Metal cleaner, clean soft cloth
SOLID TOP Weekly	1. Allow range to cool	
	2. Remove center lid	Ring hook
	3. Remove ring and side plates	Hand
	4. Spread paper on firebrick	Brown paper or newspaper
	5. Scrape off burned-on particles from lid, ring, and side plates	Paper, putty knife
	6. Scrape edges and top surface	Putty knife, wire brush
	7. Soak parts 20 to 30 minutes	Hot machine detergent solution
	8. Scrub parts, edges, and top surface	Hot machine detergent solution, gong brush
	9. Rinse, wipe dry, remove paper from firebrick	Clean hot water, clean dry cloth
	10. Reassemble all parts of the top	Hand and ring hook
	11. Apply rust preventative	Salad oil or clean shortening
BURNER GRIDS Each time frialator shortening is changed	1. Remove burner grids	
	2. Boil burner grids while cleaning frialator	Frialator solution
	3. Take to pot-and-pan sink, scrub	Hot machine detergent solution, gong brush, wire brush
	4. Rinse and wipe dry	Clean hot water, clean dry cloth
	5. Replace burner grids	

Procedure 28.   How to Clean Range Ovens

When	*How*	*Use*
Daily	1. Allow oven to cool	
	2. Remove shelf	
	3. Scrape burned particles from hearth	Long-handled metal scraper
	4. Brush out interior, shelf ledges, and door crevice	Long-handled brush
	5. Replace shelf	
	6. Wash outside of door and frame	Cloth wrung out in hot machine detergent solution
	7. Rinse and wipe dry	Clean hot water, clean dry cloth
Weekly	1. Allow oven to cool	
	2. Remove shelf, take to pot-and pan-sink, and scrub	Hot machine detergent solution, gong brush, metal sponge
	3. Rinse and wipe dry	Clean hot water Clean dry cloth
	4. Scrape burned-on particles from hearth	Long-handled metal scraper
	5. Brush interior, shelf ledges, and door crevices	Long-handled brush Dust pan
	6. Scrub interior, shelf ledges, inside and outside of door, and frame	Hot machine detergent solution, long-handled brush
	7. Rinse inside and outside of oven	Clean hot water, clean damp cloth
	8. Replace clean shelf	
	9. Wipe outside dry and polish metal trim	Clean dry cloth Metal polish

Procedure 29.   How to Clean Electric Stack Ovens

When	How	Use
Daily	1. Allow oven to cool	
	2. Scrape each deck to loosen all burned-on particles	Long-handled metal scraper
	3. Brush burned particles from each deck, starting with top deck. Give special attention to door crevice. Check to see if oven door closes properly	Long handled brush and dust pan
	4. Scrub inside and outside of each oven door	Metal sponge, gong brush, hot machine detergent solution
	5. Wash outside of oven, start with top, do sides, back, and front	Same as above
	6. Rinse and wipe dry	Clean hot water Clean dry cloth
	7. Polish any metal surfaces, handles or trim	Appropriate metal cleaner Clean soft cloth

Procedure 30.   How to Clean Gas Stack Ovens

When	How	Use
Daily	1. Allow oven to cool	
	2. Scrape each oven deck to loosen burned-on particles	Long-handled metal scraper
	3. Brush burned particles from each deck, starting with top deck. Give special attention to door crevices. Check to see if oven doors close properly	Long-handled brush and dust pan
	4. Brush out burner compartments. Light burners, check for clogged burners, if so, remove and clean	Radiator type brush Ice pick
	5. Scrub inside and outside of each oven door	Metal sponge, gong brush, hot machine detergent solution
	6. Wash outside of oven, start with top, do sides, back and front	Same as above
	7. Rinse, wipe dry	Clean hot water Clean dry cloth
	8. Polish any metal surfaces, handles, or trim	Appropriate metal cleaner and soft cloth

Procedure 31.   How to Clean Pot-and-Pan Machine

When	How	Use
After each use	1. Close steam valve or turn off gas burner	
	2. Lift overflow funnel to drain tank	
	3. Remove and empty filter screens	
	4. Scrub screens and overflow funnel in soak sink	Hot machine detergent solution, gong brush
	5. Flush interior of machine, scrub inside while flushing machine	Hose, hot water, long-handled gong brush
	6. Hose down inside of machine (this cools metal and makes it easier to remove stains)	Cold water, hose
	7. Replace overflow funnel and screens	
	8. Wipe off outside and top of machine	Hot machine detergent solution, clean cloth
	9. Rinse, wipe dry	Clean water, clean dry cloth
	10. Scrub drainboards	Hot machine detergent solution, gong brush
	11. Rinse, wipe dry	Clean water, clean dry cloth
	12. Leave doors open when not in use	
Weekly	1. Follows steps 1 to 7 in above schedule	
	2. Fill machine	Hot water, detergent
	3. Open steam valve or turn on gas burner	
	4. Start machine, allow machine to run for 30 minutes	
	5. Turn off steam valve or gas burner	
	6. Remove filter screens	
	7. Remove overflow funnel to drain machine	
	8. Scrub inside of machine while draining	Long-handled gong brush
	9. Flush machine	Cold water
	10. Replace overflow funnel and filter screens	
	11. Wipe down sides and top of machine, scrub drainboards	Hot machine detergent solution, gong brush, clean damp cloth

When	How	Use
	12. Rinse, wipe dry	Clean water, clean dry cloth
	13. Leave doors open when not in use	

Procedure 32. How to Clean Flite-Type Dishwasher

When	How	Use
After each meal	1. Pull scrap trays and curtains	
	2. Clean trays over garbage disposal	Hot water, hose, gong brush
	3. Run trays and curtains through dish machine	
	4. Turn off dish machine	
	5. Scrub down dish tables	Hose, hot water, long-handled gong brush
	6. Rinse and squeegee dish tables	Squeegee
	7. Drain machine; scrub tanks with brush while draining	Long-handled gong brush
	8. Hose down inside of machine (this cools metal and makes it easier to remove stains)	Hose, cold water
	9. Wipe soap dispenser electrodes, exterior of dispenser and machine	Clean damp cloth
	10. Wipe dry	Clean dry cloth
	11. Fill tanks and allow water to overflow for 2 to 3 minutes	
	12. Replace scrap trays, dispenser pan, and curtains	
After evening or last meal	1. Do not fill tanks	
	2. Do not replace curtains until next use	
Weekly	1. Clean machine the same as after each meal	
	2. Remove wash arms and clean free of foreign material	Long-handled bottle brush, ice pick
	3. Replace wash arms	
	4. Remove rinse jets	Long pin
	(a) Remove lime or iron deposits	
	(b) Tie rinse jets in clean cloth and place in machine	
	5. Take stainless steel equipment	

When	How	Use
	such as water fountain, splash troughs and covers, and place in machine	
	6. Turn off dispenser and final rinse	
	7. Fill machine and add detergent	Appropriate amount of detergent for each tank
	8. Run machine for 45 minutes	
	9. Clean dispenser electrodes	Damp cloth
	10. Drain machine, scrub tank while draining	Long-handled gong brush
	11. Hose down machine thoroughly	Hose, cold water
	12. Replace rinse jets	
	13. Wipe other stainless steel equipment dry and replace	Clean dry cloth
	14. Clean exterior of machine and dispenser	Damp cloth, stainless cleaner
	15. Rinse, wipe dry	Clean water, clean dry cloth
	16. Turn on dispenser and final rinse	

Procedure 33.   How to Clean Ice-Cream Cabinet

When	How	Use
After each meal	1. Cover ice cream	Carton lid or clean wax paper or film
	2. Wipe inside and outside of cabinet lid and rim of cabinet openings	Hot machine detergent solution, clean cloth
	3. Wipe front, sides, and top of cabinet	Same as above
	4. Rinse and wipe dry	Clean hot water, damp cloth, and clean dry cloth
	5. Clean dipper well	
	(a) Remove ice cream dippers and send to dishwasher	
	(b) Drain well, turn off running water	
	(c) Wash well	Hot machine detergent solution, damp cloth
	(d) Turn on water, rinse well	
	(e) Allow water to run slowly	
	(f) Replace clean dippers	

When	How	Use
Weekly	1. Cover ice cream	Carton lid or clean wax paper or film
	2. Remove ice cream to freezer	
	3. Disconnect plug from socket	
	4. Defrost freezer[a]	
	(a) Remove lids	
	(b) Place pan of hot water in each compartment	Very hot water, pans
	(c) Replace lids	
	(d) Steam for 10 to 15 minutes	
	(e) Replace water with more hot water, if necessary	
	5. Remove loosened sheets of ice or frost	Heavy spatula, pan
	6. Scrub interior, lids, rim openings, and outside of freezer	Hot machine detergent solution, gong brush, cloth
	7. Wipe up excess water	Clean dry cloth or sponge
	8. Rinse and repeat step #7	Clean hot water
	9. Wipe lids, rim openings, and outside of freezer	Clean dry cloth
	10. Connect plug to power source	
	11. Replace ice cream when temperature reaches 10°F	
	12. Replace lids	

[a] Steam hose may be used in place of hot water for defrosting.

Procedure 34. How to Clean Reach-in Refrigerator

When	How	Use
Daily	1. Check contents for any item that needs to be covered or discarded	
	2. Wipe up spills on shelves, sides, and floor	Hot machine detergent solution, clean cloth
	3. Wash doors inside and out, door frames, and front	Same as above
	4. Rinse	Clean hot water, clean cloth
	5. Wipe outside dry	Clean dry cloth
	6. Polish outside (if stainless steel)	Stainless steel polish Soft dry cloth
Weekly	1. Transfer all items to walk-in refrigerator	Cart
	2. Remove shelves, take to pot-and-pan sink[a]	Cart
	3. Scrub shelves top and bottom	Hot machine detergent solution, gong brush
	4. Rinse	Clean hot water, 170°F for 1 minute
	5. Air dry	Clean surface
	6. Scrub box inside and out give special attention to: (a) Shelf glides (b) Door frame and hinge area	Hot machine detergent solution, gong brush, clean cloth
	7. Rinse	Clean hot water, clean cloth
	8. Sanitize, allow to air dry	Cloth saturated with sanitizing solution
	9. Replace shelves	
	10. Wipe outside of box dry	Clean dry cloth
	11. Polish (if stainless steel)	Stainless steel polish, soft dry cloth
	12. Replace food items as soon as box temperature reaches 40°F	

[a] Shelves may be cleaned in dish machine or pot-and-pan machine.

Procedure 35. How to Clean Steam Table

When	How	Use
After each use	1. Turn off steam	
	2. Drain	
	3. Wash steam-table adapters,[a] surrounding frame, and overhead shelf	Hot machine detergent solution, clean cloth
	4. Rinse	Clean hot water, cloth
	5. Wipe dry and replace adaptors	Clean dry cloth
	6. Wash front and back of steam table, wipe dry	Hot machine detergent solution, clean dry cloth
	7. Polish stainless steel as needed	Stainless steel polish, soft dry cloth
Daily after evening meal	1. Turn off steam	
	2. Add detergent to water in steam table	Machine detergent
	3. Wash steam table adaptors, surrounding frame, and overhead shelf	Hot machine detergent solution, clean cloth
	4. Rinse adaptors and overhead shelf, wipe dry; lay adaptors aside	Clean hot water, cloth Clean dry cloth
	5. Scrub inside of steam table, give special attention to steam pipes and crevice below pipes	Long-handled gong brush
	6. Drain	
	7. Rinse	Clean water
	8. Wipe surrounding frame dry	Clean dry cloth
	9. Replace adaptors and covers	
	10. Wash front and back of steam table	Hot machine detergent solution, clean cloth
	11. Rinse	Clean hot water, cloth
	12. Wipe dry	Clean dry cloth
	13. Polish stainless steel as needed	Stainless steel polish, soft dry cloth

[a] Adaptors may also be washed in dish machine.

Procedure 36.　How to Clean Dish Trucks

When	How	Use
After each use	1. Wipe up any spilled material	Cloth saturated with hot machine detergent solution
	2. Rinse	Clean warm water
	3. Wipe dry	Clean dry cloth
Daily	1. Scrub top, shelves, frame	Hot machine detergent solution, gong brush
	2. Rinse	Clean warm water
	3. Sanitize top and each shelf	Cloth saturated with chemical sanitizer
	4. Air dry	
	5. Polish frames and handle	Clean dry cloth

Procedure 37.　How to Clean Baker's Table

When	How	Use
TOP AND SIDES	1. Scrape table top	Bench knife
As needed	2. Remove all scrapings and dry flour	Dry cloth, pan
throughout	3. Scrub top, sides and spice shelf	Hot machine detergent solution, gong brush
the day and		
at end of	4. Rinse	Clean hot water, clean cloth
day		
	5. Sanitize top	Clean cloth saturated with chemical sanitizer solution
	6. Air dry top, wipe sides and shelf dry	Clean dry cloth
DRAWERS	1. Remove all utensils	Clean tray
Weekly	2. Remove drawers from table (a) Press in on safety clamp	
	3. Take drawers to pot-and-pan sink	Cart
	4. Scrub drawers, inside and outside	Hot machine detergent solution, gong brush
	5. Rinse	Clean hot water, 170°F for 1 minute
	6. Dry	Clean dry cloth
	7. Wipe drawer frames	Clean damp cloth dipped into hot machine detergent solution
	8. Rinse and wipe dry	Clean hot water, clean dry cloth

When	How	Use
	9. Return drawers to table (a) Press in safety clamp to insert (b) Release safety clamp to lock (c) Test lock 10. Put clean utensils back into drawers	Cart
TABLE BINS Before refilling	1. Remove bins from table (a) Press in on safety clamp 2. Empty any remaining material into clean container 3. Vacuum each bin cavity and inside frame to remove all dry flour or sugar 4. Take bins to pot-and-pan sink 5. Scrub bins, inside and outside 6. Rinse 7. Wipe dry 8. Return to baker's table 9. Wash inside frame of table 10. Rinse 11. Wipe dry 12. Replace bins (a) Press in on safety clamp to insert (b) Release safety clamp to lock (c) Test lock 13. Refill, put new material in first	Clean container Vacuum cleaner Pallet truck Hot machine detergent solution, gong brush Clean hot water 170°F for 1 minute Clean dry cloth Pallet truck Damp clean cloth dipped into hot machine detergent solution Clean hot water, cloth Clean dry cloth

Procedure 38.   How to Clean Kitchen Tables

When	How	Use
TABLE TOPS As needed throughout the day and at the close of each shift	1. Remove any loose food particles 2. Scrub 3. Rinse 4. Sanitize 5. Allow to air dry	Clean damp cloth Hot machine detergent solution, gong brush Clean hot water, clean cloth Clean cloth saturated with chemical sanitizer solution

DRAWERS
Weekly
	1. Remove all utensils
	2. Remove drawers from table
	   (a) Press in on safety clamp
	3. Take drawers to pot-and-pan sink
	4. Scrub drawers inside and out
	
	5. Rinse
	
	6. Wipe dry
	7. Wipe drawer frames
	
	8. Rinse and wipe dry
	
	9. Return drawers to table
	   (a) Press in safety clamp to insert
	   (b) Release safety clamp to lock
	   (c) Test lock
	10. Put clean utensils back into
	    drawers
		Clean container
		
		Cart
		Hot machine detergent
		solution, gong brush
		Clean hot water, 170°F
		for 1 minute
		Clean dry cloth
		Clean damp cloth dipped
		into hot machine
		detergent solution
		Clean hot water, clean
		dry cloth
		Cart

SHELF UNDER TABLE Weekly	1. Remove everything from shelf 2. Scrub shelf 3. Rinse 4. Wipe dry 5. Replace materials on shelf	 Hot machine detergent solution, gong brush Clean hot water, clean cloth Clean dry cloth

Procedure 39.   How to Clean Metal Shelving (Pot-and-Pan Storage)[a]

When	How	Use
Weekly	1. Remove pots and pans to clean surface, place upright	Sink, drainboard, or cart
	2. Scrub top and bottom of metal shelving	Long-handled gong brush Hot machine detergent solution
	3. Rinse	Clean warm water
	4. Sanitize	Clean cloth saturated with chemical sanitizer solution
	5. Allow to air dry	
	6. Replace pots and pans, top down	

[a] Use same procedure for cleaning all metal shelving.

SECTION C

A Sound Food Supply: Purchasing and Sanitary Storage

In order for a sanitation program to be effective, it should start with a sound food supply. The person entrusted with purchasing is responsible for getting the best he can for the money he spends. To assure wholesomeness, it is of greatest importance to specify exactly what one wants. Certain government agencies concerned with the protection of our food supply are doing an excellent job for us in connection with safeguarding the wholesomeness of food. This aid is given on various levels of government—federal, state, and local.

On the federal level, the Food and Drug Administration (a unit of the U. S. Public Health Service, U. S. Department of Health, Education and Welfare) and the Department of Agriculture have established and continue to establish standards for the wholesomeness and other quality characteristics of food. The Food and Drug Administration (FDA) enforces the Food, Drug, and Cosmetic Act and it sees to it that food shipped in interstate commerce (trade across state lines), is safe, pure, and processed under sanitary conditions. The certification of shellfish is also under the jurisdiction of the Food and Drug Administration. The agency also has responsibility for the safety of food and drinking water aboard planes, trains, buses, and ships operating under the U. S. flag. The food, milk, shellfish and interstate-travel programs are all in a newly formed Division of Sanitation Control in the FDA's Bureau of Compliance.

The U. S. Public Health Service, among many other activities, has developed model sanitary standards and codes for water, milk, and other foods. It cooperates closely with industry in the production of safe and wholesome food.

The U. S. Department of Agriculture establishes and enforces food standards through its Agricultural Marketing Service. The Meat and the Poultry Inspection Branches of this service enforce the regulations for wholesomeness for meat and poultry. Federal inspectors inspect the livestock and poultry before and after slaughter to ascertain that the meat comes from healthy animals and is wholesome. The inspectors also keep a watchful eye on sanitary procedures used in the packing plants.

On the state and local levels we have definite regulations that safeguard the wholesomeness of various hazardous and highly perishable food products. The food purchaser, whether he is the proprietor or manager, should be familiar with these regulations.

Certain food items are potentially hazardous.

Some foods must be considered potentially hazardous because of their composition and/or the handling they receive. The definition of such foods by the U. S. Public Health Service* reads as follows:

"Potentially Hazardous Food shall mean any perishable food which consists in whole or in part of milk or milk products, eggs, meat, poultry, fish, shellfish, or other ingredients, capable of supporting rapid and progressive growth of infectious or toxigenic microorganisms."

We shall now discuss the particular hazards one should be alerted to when purchasing these food groups; how and for how long one should store them; what the hazards of prolonged storage are; what the signs of quality loss are; and what one should do about suspect food.

MILK AND OTHER DAIRY PRODUCTS

The composition, sanitary production, and marketing of milk is regulated by strict federal, state, and local laws. If these are properly enforced, the public can be assured of receiving a high-quality product. Only approximately 4% of all foodborne illness reported were due to milk. (See Figure 14.)

The U. S. Public Health Service has established regulations for the sanitary production and processing of fluid milk, and these are laid down in its "Milk Ordinance and Code." Most state and local regulations closely follow federal regulations. *Consult the state or local health departments for regulations that apply to the purchase and the service of milk in your food-service operation.*

In properly pasteurized milk and cream, all pathogens and the majority of other microorganisms have been killed. Pasteurization involves heating the milk to specified temperatures, holding it there for specified times, and cooling it quickly. In the holding method, the milk is heated at a temperature of 145°F for 30 minutes; in the high-temperature-short-time method, at 161°F for 15 seconds. In either case, the milk must be cooled quickly to

* U.S. Department of Health, Education and Welfare, Public Health Service. *Food Service Sanitation Manual* (see READINGS of Part II, pg. 56).

Table 3.   Safety of Milk and Other Dairy Products

Food	Potential Hazard When Purchased	Suggested Type and Length of Storage	Reason for Limited Storage	Possible Hazards Due to Handling and Prolonged Storage	Signs of Quality Loss (Spoilage)	What to Do About Suspect Foods
FLUID MILK (Fresh)	None, if pasteurized, and carton or bottle undamaged.	Refrigerate at 36 to 40°F in original container; homogenized milk can be frozen. Daily delivery recommended; store no longer than 3 days.	Properly pasteurized and packaged milk has good keeping quality for several days.	Opening of carton or other container makes milk vulnerable to contamination. Especially vulnerable is milk poured into pitchers, and then (as leftover) returned to container. Milk contaminated with staph may not appear spoiled.	At refrigerator temperature, spoilage by souring is rather rare; psychrophilic bacteria cause bitterness, proteolysis.	Discard.
BUTTERMILK, SOUR CREAM, OTHER FERMENTED MILKS	None, if pasteurized, and carton is undamaged.	Refrigerate at 36 to 40°F in original container. Several days.	Good keeping quality, due to products' acidity.	If accessible to air, mold may grow.	Off-flavor; separation; mold growth.	Discard.

CREAM (Fresh)	None, if pasteurized and carton or bottle undamaged.	Refrigerate at 36 to 40°F in original container. 1 to 3 days.	Cream spoils faster than milk.	Opening of container makes cream vulnerable to contamination. Cream contaminated with staph may not appear spoiled.	At refrigerator temperature, spoilage by souring is rare; psychrophilic bacteria cause bitterness, sliminess.	Discard.
EVAPORATED MILK (Unopened)	None, if can appears normal and has no defects.	Cool (60°F) storage preferred, especially if in large supply; after long storage, thickening may take place. Average storage is 6 to 12 months; quicker turnover recommended. Shake or turn cans periodically to prevent thickening.	In very warm, near 120°F storage, thermophilic bacteria may spoil contents.	No health hazards except if leakage occurs (bacteria can enter damaged cans).	Swelling of can; off-odor; putrefaction; discoloration; thickening.	Discard.
EVAPORATED MILK (Opened)		Refrigerate in original container. Up to 3 days.	Once can is opened, contents are vulnerable to contamination.	Handling may introduce staph and other dangerous microorganisms from hands and soiled can openers.	Off-flavor (however, poisoning bacteria may not noticeably change contents).	Discard.

Table 3. (Continued)

Food	Potential Hazard When Purchased	Suggested Type and Length of Storage	Reason for Limited Storage	Possible Hazards Due to Handling and Prolonged Storage	Signs of Quality Loss (Spoilage)	What to Do About Suspect Foods
CONDENSED SWEETENED MILK (Unopened)	None, if can appears normal and has no defects.	In cool (60°F) storage, several months.	With long, warm storage, can may corrode and milk may spoil. Generally good keeping quality due to high sugar content except if yeasts take over.	Because of high sugar content, yeasts are the main cause of spoilage; yeasts are harmless; molds may grow and may not be harmless.	Leaky cans may have contents of yeasty odor; presence of gas; mold growth.	Discard.
CONDENSED SWEETENED MILK (Opened)		Refrigerate; store up to 1 week.	Yeasts may eventually cause fermentation.	None, because of high sugar content.	Yeasty odor and flavor; bubbly, due to yeast fermentation. Mold.	Discard.
DRY SKIM MILK	None, if Grade A Milk is used, and if there is no later contamination; processing under stringent sanitary control is essential to preclude hazard.	Tightly closed in cool, dry, preferably refrigerated storage. 3 months.	When held in moist storage, there may be caking, and other quality deterioration (kitchens are warm, steamy places).	Contamination.	Stale odor, flavor; mold may be present.	If off-flavor is objectionable, discard. If moldy, discard.

RECONSTITUTED	No storage preferred; refrigerate at 36 to 40°F for no more than 1 day. Do not hold at kitchen temperature.	Chance for contamination from environment, utensils, persons handling milk. Use dry milk in powder form whenever feasible.	Contaminants may be those capable of causing foodborne illnesses.	Same as for fluid fresh milk.	Discard, if not used within safe storage time.
CHEESE 1. Cheddar type	Cheeses made from unpasteurized milk; check with local health authority about state regulations.	Refrigerate at 36 to 40°F in original wrap or closed container. Variable storage life (2 weeks to several months).	Molds may take over soon after cheese is purchased.	No danger from molds used in the processing of certain cheeses. Safety of cheeses contaminated by spoilage molds is uncertain; more needs to be known about danger from spoilage molds.	Mold growth; if surface moist, yeasts may grow and make conditions favorable for bacteria.	If cheese is very moldy (spoilage molds) discard; do not take chances.
2. Soft cheeses	Same as cheddar type.	Refrigerate at 36 to 40° F in original container. Variable storage life (3 days to 1 week; spreads, once opened, 1 to 2 weeks).	High in moisture; bacteria can grow in soft, moist cheeses.	If contaminated with staph through unsanitary handling, a hazard may exist without signs of spoilage.	Sliminess; gas production; off-odor; mold growth.	Discard.

50°F. To be labeled Grade A*, the pasteurized milk should not have a bacterial count of more than 20,000 per milliliter, and not contain over 10 coliform bacteria per milliliter. Even before pasteurization, the bacterial counts must be low. *When purchasing milk, buy Grade A.*

Milk to be served as a beverage should for sanitary reasons be purchased in individual containers filled at the creamery. Milk to be used in cooking can be purchased in 5- or 10-gallon containers. When using bulk milk, it is important to not contaminate it with soiled ladles. *Keep milk covered at all times; keep it cold.*

Whether or not milk may be dispensed for beverage purposes is a matter of law. The manager should inform himself about this matter. *If dispensing is permitted, detailed regulations must be followed regarding the care of the containers and contents, and serving procedures.* Refrigerated milk dispensers are recommended for dispensing bulk milk in kitchen and on serving line.

Milk drinks and frozen desserts like ice cream, sherbets, ice milks, and ices and mixes for frozen desserts should conform to sanitary regulations; the local health authorities should be consulted about these. In principle, all dairy products to be purchased should be processed from pasteurized milk and cream.

Properly dried milk is safe unless it is recontaminated following the drying process. Dried milk should be used in food preparation in the powder form whenever this is feasible. *Dried milk and milk reconstituted from the powder must be protected from contamination by keeping the products covered and by not contaminating them with soiled dippers and ladles.* Reconstituted milk, because of its moisture content, is as hazardous as fresh milk, or even more so, because the milk powder may have become contaminated in storage; the containers and utensils used in reconstituting the milk are not apt to be sterile; and the reconstituted product is apt to be held out of refrigeration for hours by uninformed or negligent kitchen employees. Much education of kitchen personnel needs to be undertaken to make certain that reconstituted milk is treated with as great respect as fresh milk, that is, protected from contamination and kept under constant refrigeration.

Most state health departments do not permit reconstituted milk to be served as a beverage. Consult your local health authority.

Storage

Information on type and length of storage of the various dairy products, reasons for their limited storage, possible hazards due to prolonged storage,

---

* From 1965 recommendations of the U.S. Public Health Service.

signs of quality loss, and what to do about suspect dairy foods is assembled in Table 3.

EGGS

Shell Eggs

Purchase graded, sound-shelled eggs. The shell of eggs become contaminated with bacteria, including salmonellae, during the process of laying and thereafter. If the eggs are washed, using effective, sanitary procedures, the majority of bacteria are removed. Dirty eggs are heavily contaminated.

Inside, high-quality and undamaged shell eggs are practically free from salmonellae. Unclean, cracked, and leaky eggs are dangerous. *Do not use them, ever.* In 1963 the Surgeon General of the U. S. Public Health Service issued the following statement:

"There is sufficient epidemiologic and bacteriological evidence to suggest that everyone should avoid buying and using cracked or unclean eggs. Persons who are ill, especially infants, the elderly, and individuals suffering from gastrointestinal diseases or malignancy should not be fed raw or undercooked eggs. An undercooked egg is one in which the white is not firm..."

Shell eggs are graded for size and eating quality on the basis of federal or state standards. Almost every state has legislation for egg standards, and these are fashioned after the federal models. Eggs that are graded by approved personnel and meet federal standards may carry the shield depicted in Figure 21(a).

(a)

(b)

Figure 21. Federal inspection stamp for eggs. (a) Shell eggs; (b) processed egg. (Courtesy of U.S. Department of Agriculture, Agricultural Research Service, Market Quality Research Division, Beltsville, Maryland 20705.)

Purchasing and Storing of Shell Eggs

When purchasing eggs, only eggs graded under federal-state supervision should be used. Only eggs with uncracked shells can qualify for U.S.D.A. grades. The purchaser may get assistance in writing specifications by writing to the USDA Poultry and Egg Acceptance Service.* Eggs should be kept under constant refrigeration.

Processed Eggs

Frozen eggs and dried eggs are used extensively in quantity food service. It is important that the broken-out eggs are pasteurized to kill salmonellae before they are processed. Salmonellae may contaminate the contents of the egg when the shell is broken. Purchase eggs that were processed under government supervision (see stamp, Figure 21(b).

Frozen Eggs

Store frozen eggs at 0°F. Defrost in a refrigerator and use promptly. Prevent contamination of the egg mass by keeping cans covered and using clean, sanitized dippers. *Keep under refrigeration at all times.*

Dried Eggs

Keep powder in cool, dry storage—preferably, in refrigerated dry storage. Keep cans tightly closed to keep out moisture and contaminants.

Liquid egg reconstituted from powder is highly perishable and should be used at once. Reconstituted egg should not be contaminated with hands and soiled dippers or through exposure to air, and should not be exposed to lukewarm temperatures for any length of time. *Keep refrigerated.*

From a sanitation as well as managerial point of view, it is advisable to use dried egg in powder form whenever possible rather than reconstituting it.

Storage

Information on type and length of storage of fresh and processed eggs, reasons for their limited storage, possible hazards due to prolonged storage, signs of quality loss, and what to do about suspect items is assembled in Table 4.

MEAT AND POULTRY

Buy only inspected meat and poultry. Meat and poultry should come from healthy animals, slaughtered and processed under sanitary conditions.

* Address: Poultry Division, Consumer and Marketing Service, U.S. Department of Agriculture, Washington, D.C. 20250.

Table 4.   Safety of Eggs

Food	Potential Hazard When Purchased	Suggested Type and Length of Storage	Reason for Limited Storage	Possible Hazards Due to Handling and Prolonged Storage	Signs of Quality Loss (Spoilage)	What to Do About Suspect Foods
SHELL EGGS	Slight, when eggs have clean, sound shells and are grade A or higher. Cracked eggs, especially leakers, are hazardous and man contain salmonellae; never buy dirty or cracked eggs and never use them.	Refrigeration at 36 to 40°F is required. 1 to 2 weeks.	Quality loss: absorption of odors from other foods in the refrigerator.	Penetration of bacteria through shell.	Nonmicrobial: off-odor, off flavor, thin whites, weak yolk and membranes. Microbial (if bacteria penetrated shell): cloudiness, off-color, off-odor, off-flavor.	If in doubt, discard. Discard.
EGGS BROKEN OUT OF SHELL		Refrigeration at 36 to 40°F required; use tightly covered container; strict sanitation essential. 1 day, no more.	Excellent medium for bacterial growth.	Contamination from shell of egg and from hands. Danger may exist without spoilage signs.	Whites runny; yolks have loose shape; or no signs	Discard.

Table 4. (Continued)

Food	Potential Hazard When Purchased	Suggested Type and Length of Storage	Reason for Limited Storage	Possible Hazards Due to Handling and Prolonged Storage	Signs of Quality Loss (Spoilage)	What to Do About Suspect Foods
FROZEN EGG	Recontamination after pasteurization. Buy from a reliable source.	Store at 0°F or below, up to 6 months. Defrost in refrigerator or in cold running—never warm—water. Keep under refrigeration. Use within 1 to 2 days.	Once defrosted, excellent medium for bacterial growth.	Prolonged freezer storage is no sanitary hazard. Once defrosted, danger of contamination from hands, dippers and ladles; danger of bacterial growth due to long holding in refrigeration or holding eggs in warm places during preparation hours.	There may be no obvious changes.	Discard.
DRIED EGG	No pasteurization; or recontamination after pasteurization. Buy pasteurized eggs from a reliable source.	Store in a 45°F refrigerator in tightly closed containers up to 6 months. Contents of containers, once opened, should be used	Powder in opened containers gradually absorbs moisture.	In opened containers: moldiness.	Mustiness, lumpiness, presence of mold.	Discard.

before they get lumpy.

| EGG RECONSTITUTED FROM POWDER | Use at once. 1 day storage under strict refrigeration (35 to 40°F) if storage is absolutely necessary. | Excellent medium for bacterial growth. Contaminants of reconstituted egg may stem from powder itself, unsanitary equipment, the human body, dust, and other sources. | Growth of food poisoning salmonellae, staphylococci, and other accidental contaminants. | May not show any signs. | Discard. |

Meat from diseased animals is likely to be contaminated with the animals' pathogens, which may include food-poisoning bacteria such as salmonellae and *Clostridium perfringens*. Under government inspection, diseased animals are eliminated before slaughter and all carcasses are again inspected for signs of disease after slaughter. The killing, cutting, and packing procedures are scrutinized for sanitation. The premises are inspected for clean maintenance, and the personnel for freedom from communicable diseases.

Inspection of meat and poultry shipped across state lines is under the jurisdiction of the United States Department of Agriculture. According to a recent (1967) law, every state now also requires inspection of meats sold within state boundaries; the sanitary requirements must be at least as high as those enforced for meats inspected for interstate shipment.

Meat inspected and passed for wholesomeness by federal agents carries the round mark depicted in Figure 22(a) and (b). The federal stamp for wholesomeness of poultry is shown in Figure 22(c).

Purchasing Aid given by USDA

The U. S. Department of Agriculture has both a meat and a poultry acceptance service designed especially to aid the institutional purchasers in placing orders for meat and poultry. Food service operations interested in this service may seek information by writing to the USDA.* Upon request, this service provides inspection service that allows a buyer to write his own specifications to suit his needs.

Does inspection for wholesomeness guarantee complete freedom from bacteria?

The inspection service cannot make such guarantees. Even healthy animals harbor in their intestinal tract bacteria capable of causing foodborne illnesses. Also, it must be remembered that, like humans, animals can become carriers of disease-producing germs such as salmonellae after they have recovered from the disease. Carriers look healthy. When meat animals and poultry are killed and dressed, the intestinal contents containing pathogenic bacteria may accidentally contaminate the meat. Other sources of contaminants are the employees who cut, process, and package the meat. Even healthy persons can harbor food poisoning bacteria in and on their bodies.

Which meats are most likely to be contaminated?

The extent of contamination of meat and poultry with undesirable bacteria depends on many factors: plant sanitation, working skill and habits of workers, and personal hygiene of workers—to name a few.

---

* For acceptance service, write to Consumer and Marketing Service, U.S. Dept. of Agriculture, Washington, D.C. 20250.

(a)

(b)

(c)

Figure 22. Federal inspection stamp for meat and poultry. (a) Fresh and cured meat; (b) canned and packaged meat products; (c) poultry. (Courtesy of U.S. Department of Agriculture, Agricultural Research Service, Market Quality Research Division, Beltsville, Maryland 20705.)

Contamination with bacteria is usually lowest in muscle meat and highest in ground meat, organ meats and cuts such as feet, tails, necks, and wings. Muscle meat can become contaminated in the inside when a cut is deboned and rolled. This is true for cuts like rolled rib roast as well as for turkey rolls or deboned hams. As we shall see, this fact is important to remember when preparing menu items that are meat or are made with meat (Part III, E and F).

Storage

Meat and poultry should be refrigerated separately from other foods. Information on type and length of storage of meat and meat products, and poultry and poultry products is presented in Tables 5 and 6. Given in the same table are the reasons for limited storage of these items; possible hazards due to prolonged storage; signs of quality loss; and what to do about suspect foods.

Facts to remember about meat and poultry:

1. *Purchase government-inspected meat and poultry.*
2. *Store meats and poultry by themselves. Do not store meat long, especially ground meat, organ meats, and other cuts apt to have high bacterial counts.*
3. *Expect meat and poultry to be contaminated with food-poisoning*

Table 5.   Safety of Meat

Food	Potential Hazard When Purchased	Suggested Type and Length of Storage	Reason for Limited Storage	Possible Hazards Due to Handling and Prolonged Storage	Signs of Quality Loss (Spoilage)	What to Do About Suspect Foods
FRESH MEATS (Roasts, steaks, and chops)	Presence of salmonellae, C. perfringens, fecal steptococci, Staphylococcus aureus.	Refrigerate at 30 to 36°F. Loosely wrapped meats store longer than tightly wrapped. Loosely wrapped: 3 to 5 days or less. Tightly wrapped: 2 days or less. Never keep meat at room temperature except during actual preparation.	With loose wrapping, meat surfaces are dry, retarding bacterial growth; tight wrapping causes sliminess.	Growing bacteria may not change meat noticeably even when present in high numbers.	Discoloration to brown and gray; off-odor; slight to putrid; mold growth appears late in spoilage process.	If in doubt, discard. Spoiled meat may be dangerous. Growth of salmonellae and staph not noticeable.
GROUND AND STEW MEAT	Same as steaks, roasts, and chops, except that higher bacterial count must be expected, especially in ground meat.	Refrigerate at 30 to 36°F. Freeze, unless designated for immediate use. 1 to 2 days, preferably only 1 day. Longer storage possible if original quality	Although high original quality is very important for keeping quality, all ground and-cut-up meats have an excellent chance to spoil fast.	Ground and stew meats subjected to much handling, especially ground meats; bacteria are spread throughout; grinding releases juices from meat	Same as roasts, steaks, and chops.	Same as steaks, roasts, and chops.

...ture is low (near 32°F).

meat—all these factors favor bacterial growth and there is much surface for bacteria to grow on.

VARIETY MEATS	Same as roasts, steaks, and chops.	Refrigerate at 30 to 36°F. Loosely wrapped: 1 to 2 days.	Highly perishable.	Same as steaks, roasts, and chops.	Same as roasts, steaks, and chops.	Discard.
HAMS (Tenderized, not fully cooked)	Heat-processed only to 140°F; not sterile; occasionally fecal streptococci and staphylococci (resistant to heat and salt) survive the processing.	Keep refrigerated at 30 to 36°F at all times including storage at vendor's premises. 1 week only for best quality; 1 to 3 weeks is safe, unless mishandled (left out of refrigerator).	Not sterile; highly perishable.	With prolonged storage, contaminants may build up to high numbers and staphylococci may fabricate heat-resistant toxins. Signs of these activities not noticeable.	Discoloration; off-odor; softening; mold growth, if air is available. Iridescence on sliced ham does not indicate spoilage.	If in doubt, discard. Beware of mold growth.
HAMS (Tenderized, "fully cooked"; mildly cured, sometimes	Hams are heat-processed to 150°F and not pressure-cooked; occasionally heat resistant fecal streptococci contaminate these	Refrigerate at all times (including at vendor's premises). Storage times same as above.	Not sterile; highly perishable.	With prolonged storage, contaminants may build up to high numbers.	Discoloration; off-odor; softening; mold growth if air is available.	If in doubt, discard. Beware of mold growth.

Table 5. (Continued)

Food	Potential Hazard When Purchased	Suggested Type and Length of Storage	Reason for Limited Storage	Possible Hazards Due to Handling and Prolonged Storage	Signs of Quality Loss (Spoilage)	What to Do About Suspect Foods
smoked; internal temperature of 150°F reached)	hams; although the hams may come packaged and in cans they are not sterile in the sense that pressure-cooked, canned hams are.					
BACON, CURED	Fecal streptococci contamination. Sliced bacon is handled more than slab and may receive staph during handling.	Refrigerate at 30 to 36°F, no more than 1 to 2 weeks.	Becomes moldy quite readily, especially bacon in opened packages. Bacterial spoilage found in unopened packages of sliced bacon.	Contaminants may build up to high numbers.	Off-odor; sliminess; mold.	If in doubt, discard. Do not overstock on bacon.
COLD CUTS (Including frankfurters)	Staphylococci from handling are hazard.	Refrigerate at 30 to 36°F, wrapped with some access to air. Original quality and moisture content affect keeping quality.	Sanitary hazards and keeping quality are related to sanitation practiced in processing plant and in food-service establishment.	Handling, such as slicing and wrapping, may introduce staphylococci or mold.	Discoloration; off-odor; sliminess; mold.	Discard.

High-moisture cuts: 3 to 5 days; franks, approximately a week. Hard sausage: 2 or more weeks; inspect weekly for molds.

FROZEN MEATS	Same as fresh meats.	Assures high quality.	

Freezer-store at 0°F or below. It is good to practice rapid turnover of frozen foods. The limits for storage are these: Beef, lamb: 9 to 12 months. Pork: 6 to 9 months. Veal: 4 to 6 months. Sausage, ham, slab bacon: 1 to 3 months. Beef liver: 3 to 4 months. Pork liver: 1 to 2 months.

Prolonged freezer storage does not make frozen meat unsafe, but quality suffers. Safely defrosted, the meat should be used within 24 hours of thawing; meats that have been thawed for an unknown length of time and warmed beyond 45°F are suspect, even if no spoilage signs are noticed. DO NOT REFREEZE.

Meat that accidentally has defrosted and remained thawed for unknown periods above 45°F is suspect and cannot safely be used.

Table 6. Safety of Poultry, Fish, and Shellfish

Food	Potential Hazard When Purchased	Suggested Type and Length of Storage	Reason for Limited Storage	Possible Hazards Due to Handling and Prolonged Storage	Signs of Quality Loss (Spoilage)	What to Do About Suspect Foods
POULTRY (Fresh)	Primarily, *Salmonella* contamination; staph, *C. perfringens* and fecal streptococci may be other contaminants.	Refrigerate at 30 to 36°F loosely wrapped; remove giblets from original wrap, rewrap loosely. 1 to 2 days (freeze, if storage must be extended beyond a few days).	Rapid deterioration, due to bacterial and enzyme activity.	Spoilage signs may not be evident, but salmonellae are a health hazard.	Off-odor; discoloration; sliminess.	Discard if spoiled.
POULTRY (Frozen)	Same as fresh poultry.	Freezer at 0°F or below. Chicken, 6 to 8 months. Turkey, 4 to 5 months. Giblets, 2 to 3 months.	Assures high quality.	Safely defrosted, poultry should be used soon after thawing. DO NOT REFREEZE.	Prolonged freezer storage does not make poultry unsafe, but quality suffers.	Poultry that has accidentally defrosted and remained thawed for unknown periods above 45°F is suspect and cannot safely be used.

FISH AND SHELLFISH (Fresh, frozen, or smoked)					Discard.
	If harvested from sewage-polluted waters, human pathogens may be contaminants of these foods. *Clostridium botulinum* Type E occurs in certain waters and fish may become contaminated with it. For both quality and safety, purchase from a reliable vendor.	*Fresh fish:* refrigerate, loosely wrapped, at 30 to 32°F; or pack in ice and refrigerate; or freeze if fish cannot be used within 2 to 3 days. *Fresh shellfish:* refrigerate in original, covered container; 1 to 5 days. *Frozen fish and shellfish:* hold at 0°F 4 to 6 months; shellfish, 3 to 4 months. *Smoked fish:* if to be held longer than 3 days, freeze.	*Fresh:* highly perishable; deterioration due to bacterial activity, autolysis, rancidity. *Frozen and smoked:* may become rancid. Also, *C. botulinum* Type E can multiply at refrigerator temperatures of 38°F and above.	*Refrigerated fish:* contaminants may multiply. *Frozen items:* fish and shellfish which have been thawed for unknown time and have warmed beyond 32-38°F are suspect. DO NOT REFREEZE.	*Fresh fish:* flesh softens, eyes are sunken, flesh has strong or off odor. *Smoked fish, oysters and clams:* abnormal appearance, sour odor, flavor or other off-odor.

bacteria. Therefore, use all the precautions in their preparation that are discussed throughout Part III-E and F.

FISH AND SHELLFISH

Fish and shellfish are highly perishable foods. All fish and shellfish should be bought from reputable vendors. Fresh fish should be packed in ice; frozen fish should be kept solidly frozen.

Fish and shellfish should come from unpolluted water. When raw sewage is directed into water, human intestinal pathogens such as typhoid and other intestinal pathogenic bacteria, and hepatitis virus, will contaminate the wildlife therein.

Special danger exists when seafood harvested from polluted water is eaten raw or lightly heated. Effective supervision of dangerous harvesting areas is practiced in states where the shellfish processing is an important industry. The Food and Drug Administration, U. S. Public Health Service, cooperates with states in this endeavor by certifying shippers. *Only shellfish from certified shippers should be purchased.*

Storage

Fish and shellfish should be used promptly. If they must be stored, store them briefly, and store at temperatures close to freezing, or freeze them.

Information on type and length of storage, reasons for limited storage, possible hazards due to prolonged storage, signs of quality loss, and what to do about suspect items is presented in Table 6.

CANNED FOOD

Purchase and Storage

Damaged, bulging, leaking, and rusty cans may be dangerous and should be refused. One should not do business with a vendor who dares to deliver such foods. Canned foods should be stored in a cool, dry place. Excessive heat will spoil the contents, and freezing may break the seal of cans and allow bacteria to enter the can. Among these bacteria may be types injurious to health. Rapid turnover of canned foods is advised, since the quality of all canned foods can only go down, never up.

Information on length of storage, reason for limited storage, possible hazards due to handling and prolonged storage, signs of quality loss, and what to do about suspect items is given in Table 7.

Table 7. Safety of Canned Foods and Precooked Frozen Foods

Food	Potential Hazard When Purchased	Suggested Type and Length of Storage	Reason for Limited Storage	Possible Hazards Due to Handling and Prolonged Storage	Signs of Quality Loss (Spoilage)	What to Do About Suspect Foods
CANNED FOODS	None, if commercially processed, and if cans are intact. Underprocessed, home canned, nonacid foods may contain *Clostridium botulinum* toxin.	Cool (50-60°F), dry storage. Freezing may break seal of can or jar or crack jar; leaks will allow bacteria to enter. Unless cans or jars are damaged, freezing will not make food unsafe. Maximum storage time, 1 year, but 6 months is preferable.	General decrease in quality, especially of low-acid foods. Storage at very warm temperatures allows growth of thermophilic bacteria.	Reentry of bacteria in jars and cans, due to disintegration of seals.	Color change (red foods may lighten; colored foods fade in plain tin cans). All canned goods are gradually reduced in quality if held above 50°F.	Do not taste foods in cans that leak; that are rusty, corroded or have a broken seal; or whose contents spurt out or are bubbly, off-color, or off-odor.
FROZEN PRECOOKED FOODS	Pathogens introduced from hands and equipment; delayed freezing; warm-up during thawing.	Freezer at 0°F or below. Length of storage depends on product. Do not store anything over 3 months.	Quality disintegrates at different rates in the various frozen precooked foods.	No health hazard from prolonged storage in freezer; danger arises when food thaws and warms beyond 45°F. DO NOT REFREEZE.	Dehydration; discoloration; large ice crystals.	Potentially hazardous foods that thaw and warm to 45°F are suspect. Discard.

FROZEN PRECOOKED FOODS

Purchase and Storage

Frozen precooked foods have been cooked in processing plants. If they have been prepared in a sanitary processing plant by sanitary methods of handling and if they have been frozen rapidly, and kept frozen solidly up to the time they are used, all should be well. We see that there are many "ifs." *Defrosting, whether it occurs in the vendor's storage, in transit or elsewhere, is of real danger since bacteria may resume growth once the food is thawed.*

1. Purchase frozen menu items from reliable vendors. Even products processed under *good* sanitary conditions may lose their quality and wholesomeness when they are allowed to defrost during transit or storage.
2. Do not overstock. Frozen precooked foods lose quality fast.
3. Upon delivery, move frozen items immediately into freezers maintained at 0°F or lower.

Frozen foods should remain solidly frozen at all times; this means at 0°F or, preferably, below. Information on type and length of storage, reasons for limited storage, possible hazards due to prolonged storage, signs of quality loss, and what to do about suspect food is presented in Table 7.

GENERAL RULES FOR PURCHASING SOUND FOOD SUPPLY

Purchaser

1. Inform yourself of health regulations that pertain to the foods you buy and serve.
2. Buy only from reputable vendors. It is advisable to visit the vendors' business premises and check (a) the sanitation of the facility and the food supply; (b) the handling procedures and storage conditions; (c) the adequacy and sanitary condition of refrigerators and freezers; and (d) the sanitary conditions of the trucks.
3. Assure the wholesomeness of potentially hazardous foods.

Dairy Products. Milk and cream should be pasteurized, and other dairy products should be processed from pasteurized milk and cream.

Eggs. Purchase graded, sound-shelled eggs. Frozen and dried eggs have been pasteurized before they were frozen or dried.

Meat and Poultry. Purchase government-inspected meat and poultry.

Fish and Shellfish. Buy oysters, clams, and mussels from sources approved by the state shellfish authority or certified by the state of origin. Fish purchased locally should come from vendors with a reputation for handling fresh, wholesome fish.

Canned Foods, Staples. Buy canned foods from reliable vendors. Beware of bargain goods, unless you have convinced yourself that they deserve to be called bargains. Cheap foods are often passed on to the customer because they have been damaged due to one cause or another. Damaged cans will become unsafe when microorganisms enter; staple items in sacks or cartons are in danger of being damaged through the activity of rodents and insects.

Precooked Frozen Foods. Purchase frozen foods from reputable vendors with facilities to keep frozen items in the solidly frozen state while in storage and transit. Beware of bargain goods.

GENERAL RULES FOR CHECKING AND STORAGE OF DELIVERIES

1. Personnel assigned to the task of receiving the deliveries should have the necessary storage space ready when the goods arrive.
2. Deliveries should be checked against the specifications. Perishables should be handled first.
3. Deliveries should be inspected for their condition and for signs of spoilage, damage, insect infestation and general mishandling. Spoiled, damaged, and mishandled foods should be refused.
4. Deliveries that do not go to the kitchen for immediate use should be stored at once in appropriate storage area.
5. Staples are stored in "dry storage." This area should be:
   (a) Above grade level to protect it from danger of flooding.
   (b) Free from overhead water or sewer pipes to guard against danger of dripping water or sewage.
   (c) Free from floor drains to guard against danger from backup of waste materials, including sewage.
   (d) Cool, dark, well ventilated, and lighted.
   (e) Well maintained—neat and orderly.
   (f) Free from insects and rodents.
   (g) Provided with platforms, shelves, racks, bins, or dollies, that raise the food above floor level to guard against contamination and danger from flooding; and for easy cleaning of the floor.
   (h) Sufficiently roomy to avoid crowding of food and food contact with the wall.
   (i) Provided with brooms and waste receptacles.

6. Perishables are stored under refrigeration, either in chilled storage (refrigerators) or in freezers. Some important requirements are:

   (a) Separate refrigerators should be provided for dairy products and eggs; meat, poultry and fish; fruits and vegetables; and cooked foods.

   (b) Cold storage should be sufficiently ample to accommodate all food at peak periods such as long weekends and holidays; accommodate frozen items to be defrosted (frozen eggs, roasts, turkeys, hams, etc.); and answer the heavy demands of summer weather.

   (c) There should be sufficient shelving to assure that even at peak periods the refrigerated materials may be spread out for good air circulation and rapid cooling.

   (d) Cold storage should be placed conveniently. If this is not feasible for long-time storage, additional refrigerators should be provided near the area of food preparation. These refrigerators would be used for items used within the working day. *Refrigeration that is not easily accessible will not be used by a cook or baker.*

   (e) Thermometers should be installed in every refrigerator and checked frequently and regularly.

   (f) Metal containers should be provided for storing food items in a sanitary manner. Storing food in cartons, wooden crates, bushel baskets, and the like is an undesirable, unsanitary practice.

   (g) Food should not be placed directly on shelves plated with cadmium; this metal may cause food poisoning.

   (h) Food should not be crowded.

   (i) Shelves must not be lined with paper, cardboard, and the like because these products hinder circulation of air.

Responsibilities of management are to:

   (a) Provide sufficient, adequate storage for chilled and frozen foods.

   (b) Provide refrigeration and shelving that permit good air circulation.

   (c) Keep refrigerators and freezers in good working order.

   (d) Provide directions for cold storage of various foods to the employees.

   (e) Have refrigerators and freezers routinely cleaned and defrosted.

   (f) Check coolers and freezers for orderly arrangement, cleanliness, and lack of crowding.

   (g) Check for cleanliness of the surrounding area.

   (h) See to it that food is rotated; the new supply should go to the back and previously stored items to the front so that they will be used first.

Responsibilities of employees are to:

(a) Store the various foods in the space designated for them.

(b) Store food according to the directions provided by management.

(c) Avoid crowding the refrigerators with food; air circulation is necessary for rapid cooling.

(d) Not clutter refrigerators and freezers with unwanted items that are eventually discarded anyhow.

(e) Keep refrigerators orderly and neat, wipe up spills, etc.

(f) Not place trays directly on other foods; tray bottoms may contaminate food, and, air circulation is hampered.

(g) Follow a schedule and directions, provided by management, to clean and defrost refrigerators regularly.

The Sanitation-Conscious Food Handler:
His Health, Personal Hygiene, Work
Habits, Interests, and Attitude

The health of the food handler plays an important part in sanitation. Food handlers can be sources of bacteria causing illness in others through transmission of disease germs, or through food poisoning.

Experience has shown that a great number of foodborne illnesses come from workers who were ill, practiced poor personal hygiene, or applied unsanitary food-preparation methods. When food poisoning or food infection strikes us down, usually our food had been contaminated through the food handler's sneeze, or through pus from his infected wounds or pimples, or through fecal matter clinging to his hands.

Even the healthy person may harbor food-poisoning bacteria in his nose, mouth, throat, and intestinal tract. Therefore, the personal hygiene of a food handler is of great sanitary importance. Personal hygiene refers to the cleanliness of a person's body.

A food handler's hand habits and working habits are important in connection with sanitation. Undesirable hand habits during food preparation are scratching one's head, arranging one's hair, or touching one's nose or mouth (Figure 11). Thereby, bacteria from the person's body are transferred to food and sow the seed of food poisoning. Also, a person's clean or sloppy working habits can make the difference in reducing or increasing the chances of spreading bacteria in the kitchen.

A food handler's interest in sanitation and cooperative attitude are of extreme importance in practicing sanitation. To be interested, he must first learn about sanitation; he must understand what it is, what lack of sanitation does, and what good sanitation can do. And he must understand, and be impressed by, the fact that *he, the food handler, plays an important part in the practice of sanitation. When applying what he has learned, he*

146

must become convinced of the fact that his supervisor sees and appreciates this.

HEALTH AND PERSONAL HYGIENE OF EMPLOYEES

Management and employees should cooperate in the effort to keep ill employees from working with food and with equipment and utensils used in preparing and serving food. Examples of important human illnesses that may be transmitted through food are diseases of the respiratory tract such as the common cold, sore throat, scarlet fever, tonsillitis, pneumonia, trench mouth, sinus infections and tuberculosis (Table I, Appendix). Other diseases that may be transmitted are intestinal disorders such as typhoid fever, dysentery, Asiatic cholera, and infectious hepatitis (Table II, Appendix). In some of these diseases the germs may remain with the person after he has recovered; he may be a carrier without knowing this.

In the Food Service Sanitation Manual of the Public Health Service,[*] the following requirement regarding the health of food service personnel is given:

"No person while affected with any disease in a communicable form, or while a carrier of such disease, or while afflicted with boils, infected wounds, sores, or an acute respiratory infection, shall work in any area of a food service establishment in any capacity in which there is a likelihood of such person contaminating food or food-contact surfaces with pathogenic organisms, or transmitting disease to other individuals; and no person known or suspected of being affected with any such disease or condition shall be employed in such an area or capacity. If the manager or person in charge of the establishment has reason to suspect that any employee has contracted any disease in a communicable form or has become a carrier of such disease, he shall notify the health authority immediately."

This regulation is stringent indeed and may serve as model. It would be difficult to carry it out exactly to the letter of the law. But it should be heeded as closely as is feasible. For example, a person recovering from a cold might be permitted to return to work provided he does not handle food or utensils used in food preparation and service. The manager or supervisor should make it clear to the employee that he is not punished by being sent home or temporarily shifted to another—perhaps more

* U.S. Dept. of Health, Education and Welfare, Public Health Service *Food Service Sanitation Manual* (see *Readings of Part III*, pg. 189-190)

menial—job. The employee should understand that he is doing this for the good of the "cause," which is sanitary food service.

Responsibilities of management are to:

1. Require of a new employee that before he starts working he have a physical examination to show whether he has an acute communicable illness or is a carrier of a communicable disease.
2. Keep a watchful eye on employees for signs of illness that might be of a contagious nature; and for the presence of infections such as infected burns, sores, and boils.
3. Require a physical examination of an employee after he has been ill with a communicable disease and before he resumes work to assure that he has not become a carrier.
4. Stimulate employees to become health-conscious; educate them to hear about and understand certain basic facts about health; encourage employees to report to their supervisors any respiratory infections and gastrointestinal upsets they may have. Here, an ounce of prevention is worth a pound of cure. In many ailments, the first stages of illness are the very infectious ones; also, prompt care and bed rest usually favors faster recuperation of the patient and his return to work.
5. Provide the facilities that are essential for the employees to keep themselves clean.
   (a) Provide dressing rooms equipped with lockers, sinks, soap, and paper towels or an air dryer. Have the rooms cleaned regularly; inspect them regularly.
   (b) Provide uniforms, laundering services, or both.
   (c) Provide hand-washing sinks in the kitchen, hot water (preferably with knee-controlled or foot-controlled valves), soap, and paper towels or hand dryers.

Responsibilities of employees are to:

1. Keep themselves in good health. A healthy person feels energetic, sleeps well, performs his work without undue fatigue, has lustrous hair, clear skin, is free from respiratory and gastrointestinal disorders and other physical ailments.
2. Be health-conscious; learn about certain health facts; learn how their own health may affect that of others; they will be surprised and pleased to see how important their knowledge about health, and their attitudes about practicing good health habits, can be to the welfare of others.
3. Report to their supervisor when they have been injured, including

minor injuries such as cuts and burns. Report to him any skin eruptions, boils, and the like.

4. Report to their supervisor any abnormal condition of their respiratory system (head cold, sinus infection, sore throat, tonsillitis, bronchial and lung disorders) and intestinal disorders, such as diarrhea.

5. Report to their supervisor if the supply of soap or towels in washrooms is low or gone.

6. Practice personal cleanliness.

    (a)   Take a bath or shower daily.

    (b)   Use a deodorant.

    (c)   Wash hair at least once a week and keep it neat.

    (d)   Keep nails clean, neat, and well-trimmed.

    (e)   Wear clean undergarments daily.

7. Prepare themselves for work in a systematic fashion.

    (a)   Brush and comb their hair.

Yes   No   Yes   No

Yes   No   Yes   No

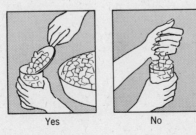

Yes   No

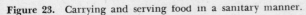

Figure 23. Carrying and serving food in a sanitary manner.

   (b) Don a hairnet (women) or cap (men).

   (c) Get into clean, comfortable shoes.

   (d) Change into their uniform; hang street clothes in the locker; do not hang clothes in the toilet or kitchen.

   (e) Clean hands and fingernails thoroughly. Wash hands with plenty of hot water and soap and dry hands on disposable towels or before an air dryer.

8. When at work, control bad hand habits. Do not scratch head or other body parts, arrange their hair, stroke their moustache, pick pimples, and so forth. If they accidentally do these things, they should wash their hands afterwards.

9. Avoid coughing or sneezing.

10. Wash their hands frequently and every time after having performed one of these activities:

   (a) Visited the toilet.

   (b) Coughed or sneezed into hands or handkerchief.

   (c) Smoked; the saliva from the butt of the cigaret or cigar will contaminate the hands.

   (d) Handled boxes, crates, packages, and other soiled articles.

   (e) Handled raw meat, poultry, shell eggs, fish, or shellfish.

   (f) Handled garbage.

   (g) Handled money.

   (h) Handled anything soiled.

Yes   No   Yes   No

Yes   No   Yes   No

Figure 24. Sanitary handling of china, glasses and flatware.

11. Keep hands and fingers out of food; do not taste food from fingers; use a clean tasting spoon each time.

12. Use utensils for preparing food as much as is feasible. Use tongs, spoons, forks, etc., for handling ice, butter, rolls, breads, pastries, etc., instead of using hands (Figure 23). Be sure the utensils are clean.

13. Observe "no smoking" rule in areas of food preparation and service.

14. Avoid touching parts of china and eating utensils that will be touched by the customer's mouth. Pick up serving and eating utensils by their handles, and glasses by their bases (Figures 23, 24).

15. Handle plates in a sanitary manner; the thumb should touch the rim of the plate only, never the plate itself or the food on it. Use plates under bowls.

16. Use plastic disposable gloves if food must be manipulated by hand. Dispose of used gloves.

Sanitary Procedures of Preparing and Holding Food: General Principles

The wholesomeness of prepared food can and must be safeguarded through sanitary practices in kitchen and storage areas, which includes effective control of food temperatures at all times.

In sanitary food service only clean, safe food is served to the public.

We have described earlier how the facility, equipment, utensils, dishes, glasses, and tableware are cleaned. We have shown ways for the purchase of a sound food supply and its sanitary storage. We shall now be concerned with the following aspects of sanitary practice:

(a) Sanitary methods of handling food in the kitchen.
(b) Safe holding of food at various temperatures.
(c) Safe cooking procedures.
(d) Safe cooling procedures.

To safeguard the wholesomeness of finished menu items at the time they are served, the following rules need to be observed:

Rule I. Start out with wholesome food material.

Rule II. Remove dirt, soil, and chemical residues by thorough washing.

Rule III. Protect food from contamination with poisonous substances and disease-producing bacteria throughout its preparation, storage, and service.

Rule IV. Thoroughly heat those foods that can be expected to harbor illness-producing microorganisms, whenever this is feasible.

Rule V. Prevent multiplication of microorganisms in the food and on equipment used in its preparation, storage, and service.

Rules I, III, and V are applicable to all menu items. Rule II is particularly important in the case of fruits and vegetables eaten raw. Rule IV can only be applied to items that tolerate thorough heating. For example,

152

a meat stew is always heated to a simmer or boil (which is thorough heating) in routine cooking. Hollandaise would curdle if thoroughly heated; and, of course, salads cannot be heated at all.

Practice Rule I—Start Out With Wholesome Materials

Follow the suggestions given above (Part III-C).

Practice Rule II—Wash Food to Remove Soil

Which Foods. Not all foods can or need to be washed. However:
· Wash all fruits and vegetables to be eaten raw
· Wash fresh vegetables to be cooked
· Wash dried fruit and raisins
· Wash raw poultry, fish and variety meats; the body cavity of poultry is especially rich in salmonellae capable of causing food poisoning

How to Wash. Fruits and vegetables. Use lukewarm running water. Wash fresh greens thoroughly to remove every bit of dirt. Rinse washed products with cold running water and drain.

In case of suspected insect infestation, soak fresh vegetables in cold salted water for 20 minutes. Salt will cause insects to rise to the top of the water.

Poultry, Fish, and Variety Meats. Wash items shortly before cooking them. Use lukewarm water followed by a cold rinse. Drain well. If items are not to be cooked immediately, keep them chilled until the time for cooking has come.

Practice Rule III—Protect Food From Contamination

Contamination of food with poisonous substances and certain types of bacteria may cause food poisoning in persons eating such contaminated food.

A. Contamination From Poisonous Substances Other Than Bacterial Toxins. Most commonly involved are chemicals that get into food by mistake. Among them are cleaning compounds, polishes, insect powders, and the like (see Part II-D).

Protective Measures. All chemicals must be stored separately from food, never in the kitchen, pantry, and other places where food is handled and stored. *There is no excuse for slipshod housekeeping.*

B. Contamination From Bacteria Capable of Causing Foodborne Illnesses. In order to understand the reasons for prescribing certain protective measures in the handling of food, the material presented in Part II, Sections B and C should be carefully read. Here are some important facts in brief that underlie procedures devised to protect our food:

· Germs causing communicable (or catching) disease may be passed on from one person to others by way of food. Therefore, *persons ill with such diseases must not be allowed to handle food; the same holds true for carriers.* Carriers are persons who harbor disease-producing bacteria, although they appear healthy.

· Germs capable of causing food poisoning frequently originate from the body of the food handlers, although other sources are rodents, flies, and cockroaches. Still others are foods of animal origin such as meat, poultry, and shellfish. Finally, soil and kitchen dust may harbor food poisoning bacteria.

· Food-poisoning bacteria from the above sources will in turn contaminate work surfaces, equipment, and utensils used in the preparation, service, and storage of ingredients and prepared menu items.

Protective Measures

Management and food handlers must fully cooperate in making sanitary measures work. Sanitary rules must be set up that are sound as well as practical. The employees must be trained in following them and must be supervised in practicing them. Everyone must see his own role in the important task of preparing food the sanitary way.

Management has the obligation to:

1. Be informed on the dangers of unsanitary practices in food preparation and service and convinced of the importance of sanitary food handling in the establishment.
2. Provide a clean facility.
3. Provide the sanitary equipment necessary for doing a sanitary job.
4. Provide utensils for tasks, which can be successfully used in place of hands, such as forks, tongs, and spoons; and see to it that these are kept clean.
5. Provide plastic gloves for tasks that may require the human hand, such as the mixing of salads, the shaping of meat or fish patties, and the like; see to it that gloves are always available so they will not be used twice and that gloves are used for one task only, and discarded after use.
6. Educate the food handler in the fundamentals of sanitation in food service and train him in the appropriate techniques.
7. Set up directions for employees to follow.
8. Provide supervision.
9. Keep food handler's interest alive through praise for jobs he does well and through constructive criticism when he fails. However, when a food handler, after careful training, consistently fails to use

sanitary techniques, he is not the person to keep in the food department.

The food handler has the obligation to:

1. Be willing to be educated in the fundamental facts about sanitation in food service on which sanitary practice is based.
2. Understand that he plays a very important role in the total sanitary program of the establishment.
3. Understand that he—a healthy person—is likely to carry food poisoning bacteria on and in him and does his best to keep these bacteria out of the food he prepares.
4. Be willing to learn sanitary techniques and use them without fail, all hours of the working day.
5. Be health-conscious, of clean appearance, and practice good personal hygiene; report to his supervisor any signs of an oncoming illness such as sore throat, head cold, flu, nausea and diarrhea, and the presence of infected sores, burns, or other infections on his body.
6. Keep undesirable hand habits under control such as fingering his nose, hair, moustache, or other body parts.
7. Refrain from sneezing or coughing onto food; sneeze or cough into a handkerchief or—in case of "surprise attack"—into his hands. *In either case he immediately washes hands to remove dangerous bacteria.*
8. Understand that a visit to the toilet will contaminate his hands with dangerous bacteria; therefore, he washes hands thoroughly before he returns to work.
9. Understand that handling raw meats, poultry, sea food and shell of eggs may deposit harmful bacteria on his hands, and wash hands before he touches other foods.
10. Understand that hands need to be washed frequently throughout the working day, and immediately after handling soiled articles.
11. Use clean, sanitary equipment.
12. Keep work surfaces clean and orderly, clean up spills promptly.
13. Keep hands out of food as much as is possible and use appropriate clean utensils instead.
14. Use gloves whenever their use is prescribed by management.
15. Never use a tasting spoon twice.
16. Always touch spoons, knives, forks and other eating utensils by the handles, glasses by their bases, cups by their handles, plates by their rims.
17. In serving never stack dishes in such a way that the areas touching the customer's lips become contaminated.

18. Prevent cross-contamination of bacteria during preparation of food (see remaining items on list).
19. Use, whenever possible, separate cutting boards, blocks, tables, grinders, slicers and other utensils for raw and cooked food.
20. If same equipment and utensils must be used, thoroughly clean and sanitize equipment used for raw food after each use.
21. Thoroughly wash hands after handling raw food.
22. When storing food, arrange it so bottoms of containers (pans, trays, and pots) will not contaminate food stored underneath, since containers that have touched unsanitary surfaces are loaded with bacteria. If one food is stored above another, bottoms of containers must be sanitary.
23. Protect food from dust, flies, cockroaches, and rodents.
24. Never leave food out overnight.
25. Cover food except when it is actually manipulated.

Practice Rule IV—Thoroughly Heat All Foods That May be Expected to Harbor Illness-Producing Microorganisms, Whenever This Is Feasible

The following foods may be expected to harbor illness-producing microorganisms:

Group 1. Raw meat—because of contamination with salmonellae and *C. perfringens.*

Group 2. Raw poultry—because of contamination with salmonellae.

Group 3. Cracked shell eggs and recontaminated processed egg—because of salmonellae.

Group 4. All items, raw or cooked, that have been subjected to manipulation by hand or machinery, because of contamination with staph, salmonellae, and perfringens bacteria; these organisms may stem from the food handler, soiled equipment and utensils; raw meat and poultry; and egg shells.

Temperatures to which items should be heated to kill dangerous microorganisms.

Heating to at least 165°F is necessary to kill bacteria that do not form spores, such as staph, salmonellae, and streptococci. Trichinae will also be killed by such heating. However, the spores of perfringens bacteria are resistant to heat and require temperatures higher than 165°F for kill.

Menu items that in routine cooking are heated to safe temperatures at site of contamination.

Group 1.   *Meats.*   (a) Items that are boiled, stewed, braised, steamed, broiled, and panbroiled are safe.

(b) Roasts that have not been boned and roasts that were boned but not rolled are also safe even if heated to the rare stage; the meat is sterile on the inside, and outside bacteria are killed.

(c) Trichinae are killed in pork roasted to the gray stage (170°F).

Caution: Boned, rolled roasts, gravies and items that are made from ground meat may be unsafe.

Group 2. *Poultry.* **(a)** Items that are boiled, stewed, fricasseed, braised, steamed, broiled, and panbroiled are safe.

(b) Roast poultry is safe (except large stuffed turkey).

Group 3. *Eggs and egg-thickened products.* **(a)** Hard cooked eggs are safe.

(b) Souffles are safe.

(c) Baked custards are safe.

Group 4. *Items that have undergone much handling (grinding, chopping, or mincing).* These items are safe only *if* cooked to the "done" stage (hamburger) or are heated to boiling temperatures all the way through (casseroles, meat pies, poultry pies and the like).

Caution: These items are frequently underheated and are therefore discussed in Part III-F.

Menu items that in routine cooking cannot be heated to safe temperatures because they would lose appeal or are not heated to safe temperatures for other reasons.

Group 1. *Meat and gravy.* **(a)** Boned, rolled roasts heated to the rare and medium rare stage are hazardous. The inside of the roast is likely to become contaminated during deboning, and the inside does not get sufficiently hot for bacteria, especially spores, to be killed.

(b) Gravies may or may not be safe. The danger exists that gravies may become contaminated with perfringens bacteria from meat juice released from the inside of rolled rare roasts. Boiling the finished gravy will make gravies safe, unless the spores are of the heat-resistant type.

(c) Items made with ground meat are hazardous unless cooked to the gray (done) stage.

(d) Hams may be unsafe unless heated to at least 165°F, preferably 170°F.

Group 2.   *Poultry.*   (a) Large (18 pounds and over) roast turkeys that are stuffed are unsafe because heat penetration is slow into the center of the stuffing. Large turkeys should never be stuffed.

Group 3.   *Eggs and*   Lightly heated are:
egg-thickened   (a) Soft cooked eggs. Therefore, use
products.   sound-shelled eggs.

(b) Scrambled eggs. Use sound-shelled fresh or pasteurized processed egg.

(c) Omelets cooked on top of the stove. Use sound-shelled fresh eggs or pasteurized processed egg.

(d) Stirred custards—use sound-shelled fresh eggs or pasteurized processed egg.

(e) Egg-thickened items that are not really hot when the egg is incorporated (stirred custards, puddings, and cream fillings). Use proper heating procedure (Part III-F).

(f) Meringue pies. Use proper heating procedure (Part III-F).

Group 4.   *Certain items*   (a) Deep-fried items such as croquettes
that have under-   routinely receive light heat treat-
gone much   ment.
handling.   (b) Pan-fried patties like crab cakes and

fish cakes routinely receive light heat treatment.

(c) Meat pies, poultry pies, and casseroles (freshly made-up or frozen) are frequently underheated by default.

(d) Creamed items are frequently underheated by default.

(e) Leftovers to be served hot are frequently underheated by default.

(f) Cream-filled pastries.

Summary of recommendations on heating foods that may be expected to harbor illness-producing microorganisms:

1. Items that are improved by, or can tolerate without quality loss, high heat should be heated to at at least 165°F to be rendered safe (although spores of perfringens bacteria cannot be expected to be killed at 165°F).

   There is no excuse for underheating by default (carelessness, poor planning, or negligence.)

2. Special heating procedures can be used for certain items to assure that dangerous bacteria are killed in the cooking process. The student is referred to Part III-F.

3. In cases where heating adequately to kill bacteria is not possible, protective measures other than application of "killing heat" must be used to assure that the items are safe when served. If we cannot kill the dangerous bacteria, we must—without fail—prevent them from multiplying (see Rule V).

Practice Rule V—Prevent Multiplication of Microorganisms

We do not live in a sterile world. Bacteria are everywhere. Even if we use care and try to prevent contamination of the menu items we serve, some bacteria will probably find their way into the food and contaminate it. *We must prevent the multiplication of contaminants at every step of food preparation.*

1. During actual manipulation in preparation.
2. During hot-holding of prepared food.
3. During chilling of prepared food.
4. In handling of frozen food.

Temperatures at which bacteria multiply or merely survive, or die, are given in Figure 25.

Bacteria capable of causing foodborne illnesses multiply over a wide

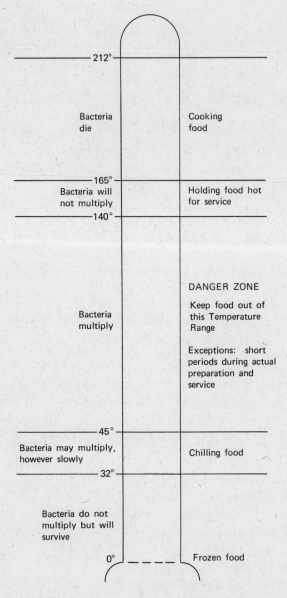

Figure 25. Food temperatures at which bacteria multiply, survive, and die.

range of temperature. The range of 45 to 140°F is called the DANGER ZONE because the hazard of bacterial growth is great within that range. The longest period for which food may safely remain in this zone is 4 hours; but food should not be in the 60 to 120°F range longer than 2 hours. These time periods are cumulative. This means that every minute that the food has remained at these dangerous temperatures counts toward these 4 hours and 2 hours, respectively.

Hazardous food temperatures may be created under a great variety of circumstances. Here are some examples:

· Frozen items left to thaw in the kitchen.
· Perishable ingredients, semiprepared menu items, and fully prepared items exposed to warm kitchen temperatures.
· Cooked food held lukewarm in uncontrolled hot-holding equipment.
· Perishable items displayed on buffet tables, cold food getting too warm and hot foods too cool for safety.
· Food refrigerated in large batches.

1. Prevent Multiplication of Bacteria in Food While it is Actually Manipulated During Preparation. Remember that kitchens are warm places, the air temperature there being approximately 20 to 30 degrees higher than the temperature of other rooms. Therefore, reduce to a minimum the time for which food is exposed to kitchen temperatures.

Recommendations

Management has the obligation to:

1. Plan the employee's work so exposure of food to warm temperatures is reduced to the period of actual manipulation.
2. If at all possible, provide cool rooms for the preliminary preparation of hazardous items involving meat, poultry, fish, and shellfish.
3. Instruct workers to prepare salads and sandwiches from chilled ingredients.
4. Provide refrigeration in the area of food preparation for the temporary storage of partly prepared, hazardous items and for hazardous ingredients such as frozen egg, reconstituted egg, and reconstituted milk.
5. Provide supervision.

The food handler has the obligation to:

1. Follow preparation procedures laid down by management.
2. Endeavor to keep hazardous food items either hot or cold.
3. Cooperate in every way with management in keeping hazardous foods

out of the DANGER ZONE—except when food is actually manipulated.

2. Prevent Multiplication of Bacteria in Food Being Held Hot until Served. Remember that regardless of whether hot food is held in the original cooking equipment, or in special hot-holding equipment, *food temperatures must be maintained at 140°F or higher.*

Heated holding equipment is designed for hot-holding, not for heating; therefore, food must be hot, preferably 165°F or above, when transferred to the hot-holding equipment.

Recommendations

Management has the obligation to:

1. Provide hot-holding equipment that keeps food at a minimum temperature of 140°F, and maintain equipment in good working order.
2. Plan food production in such a way that hot food remains in the heated holding equipment for the shortest time feasible.
3. Checks food temperatures frequently with a thermometer in center of batch to ensure that:
    (a) Food is at least 165°F when placed in heated holding equipment.
    (b) Food is kept hot (at least 140°F) throughout holding.
4. See to it that food that receives much handling followed by light heating in routine cooking is consumed within a short time. This involves *staggered preparation* of items such as:
    (a) Creamed meat, poultry, fish, and shellfish.
    (b) Ground meat patties cooked to the rare or medium stage.
    (c) Crab and fish cakes.
    (d) Croquettes and other lightly-heated products.

The food handler has the obligation to:

1. Fully cooperate with management in the important task of holding hot food hot.
2. Take care to have food hot (at least 165°F) all the way through before it is placed in the heated holding equipment.
3. Use good judgment when preparing items by "staggered" operation; keep production just ahead of demand.

3. Prevent Multiplication of Bacteria in Chilling Food. Remember, that the food temperature that must be reached in order to chill food safely is 45°F or lower, and that this temperature should be reached as soon as possible, since the food should not be in the DANGER ZONE (140°F to 45°F) longer than a total of 4 hours, at the most.

Speed of cooling is affected by many factors:
- Liquid foods cool faster than solid foods.
- Small batches cool faster than large ones.
- Shallow layers cool faster than deep ones (Figure 26).
- Items exposed to low refrigerator temperatures (well below 40°F) cool faster than those exposed to refrigerator temperatures above 40°F.

Cooling food at room temperature is a dangerous practice because foods will cool slowly and temperatures inviting bacterial growth will prevail for a long time. Chances for contamination add to the danger.

The notion is false that food placed in a refrigerator while warm will turn sour because "heat is sealed in."

Recommendations for Chilling

Management has the obligation to:

1. Provide refrigeration equipment sufficient for fast chilling to safe temperatures of all foods requiring refrigeration.
2. See to it that specific refrigerators are used only for the food designated

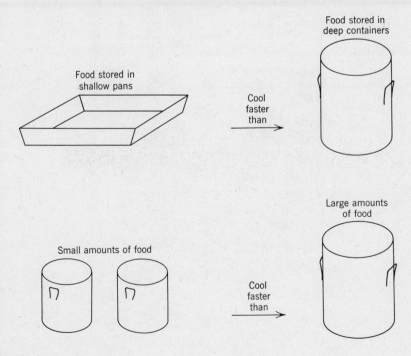

Figure 26. Chilling food.

for these refrigerators; for example, meat separated from other items and cooked items separated from raw foods.

3. Provide refrigeration in locations where it can be easily reached by employees; only then *will* it be used.

4. See to it that refrigerators are in good working order, and that repairs, when necessary, are made promptly. See to it refrigerators are kept clean, orderly, uncluttered. Have equipment checked at routine intervals by a reliable serviceman.

5. Provide ample shelving and portable wire racks (Figure 27) to avoid stacking of containers. Stacking causes contamination and interferes with the circulation of air.

6. Provide floor racks for walk-in coolers; food should not be stored on floor.

7. See to it that each refrigerator can handle its designated load and that the refrigerator temperature remains low and safe at peak load. Several thermometers should be installed in each refrigerator and read daily;

Figure 27.   Movable rack for chilling food. (Reprinted from B. B. West et al., *Food Service in Institutions,* 4th ed., 1966, by permission of John Wiley & Sons, New York.)

if only one thermometer is used, it should be so installed that it registers in the warmest area of the refrigerator.

8. Provide additional refrigeration if persistently high temperature reading indicate that refrigeration facilities are insufficient.
9. Provide equipment for rapid precooling food outside the refrigerator.
10. Set up appropriate and efficient precooling procedures. The combined cooling time to 45°F outside and inside the refrigerator should be achieved within 4 hours at the most, and preferably in less time.
11. Set up guidelines for refrigeration of the various items.
12. Provide supervision.
13. Give directions for length of storage, and use of leftovers.

The food handler has the obligation to:

1. Fully cooperate with management in the important task of cooling food rapidly to safe temperatures.
2. Protect food from contamination during cooling.
3. Avoid opening the refrigerator doors unnecessarily often.
4. Avoid allowing the door to remain open for extended periods of time.
5. Keep refrigerator in good order and clean up spills immediately.
6. Refrain from stacking containers on top of each other because of the danger of contamination from soiled container bottoms.
7. Precool food, whenever required, by methods prescribed by management.
8. Use leftovers as directed.

Foods that Need to be Chilled

All potentially hazardous items require rapid chilling and continuous cold-holding whether they are raw, partially or fully prepared in advance, or leftovers.

Hot leftovers that tolerate reheating to boiling should be brought to a boil to destroy contaminants, then chilled rapidly and refrigerated. This rule applies in particular to items that come back from the counter, buffet tables, patient floors, and the like.

GUIDELINES FOR CHILLING FLUID ITEMS AND FLUID ITEMS THAT WILL THICKEN ON COOLING

Small Batches. Distribute food into 1 or 2 gallon containers and refrigerate. Do not cool food at room temperatures, except possibly for the first half hour after the heat is turned off. Use shallow pans for puddings and other items that thicken on cooling. Allow to cool uncovered for the first 30 minutes, then cover.

Large Batches. Because heat leaves large batches slowly, precool food to approximately 80°F; use agitation to hasten cooling.

· Use a cooling kettle with slowly rotating scraper-agitation. Or use stock-pots (2 or 4 gallons) immersed in cold running water; agitate with a suitable utensil every 20 to 30 minutes to mix contents well.

· Refrigerate food in 2 or 4 gallon batches. Use shallow pans for puddings and other items that thicken on cooling; or (if desired) distribute food into individual serving dishes, set on trays, set trays on racks (Figure 27), and refrigerate.

· Creamed foods and other items that are mixtures of fluid and solid foods must be handled gently when agitated, lest the solid pieces break up and the consistency of the item be marred.

GUIDELINES FOR CHILLING SOLID ITEMS

· Plan for large roasts, baked hams, and turkeys to be done just before being served; they cool slowly, reheat slowly, and do not lend themselves to advance preparation because of danger from bacterial growth.

· Leftover large roasts, hams, and turkeys will cool faster if cut into smaller portions, sliced (roasts, hams), or disjointed (turkeys), the slices and pieces being then arranged in shallow layers on trays. This practice has its limitations, due to undesirable changes in quality during reheating.

· Always cool meat separately from gravy. For cooling of gravy, see the guidelines for chilling fluid items.

· Whole steamed or simmered turkey cools slowly. Therefore, cut turkeys in half lengthwise prior to cooking. Cool in single layers. Better still, disjoint them and cool in small pieces, single-layered.

· Debone meat and poultry as soon as it is sufficiently cool for handling; bones interfere with cooling. Meat and poultry may be deboned before cooking. This has the advantage of (a) permitting faster cooling and (b) reducing the danger of contamination, which comes from handling the cooked meat.

· Suggestions for safe refrigeration of various hazardous menu items and precautions in the use of leftovers are given in Part III-F.

Length of Chilled Storage

Facts to remember:

1. Storage does not improve cooked food; the contrary is true.
2. Even when food is held at properly low temperature (40°F or below), cold-loving bacteria may spoil the food. Dangerous bacteria may multiply, although slowly.

3. Leftovers are usually subjected to various cycles of holding (heating—hot-holding—chilling) and are likely to be subjected for many hours to temperatures at which bacteria may multiply. In leftovers that are reheated before they are stored, the majority of bacteria are killed. Still, all leftovers are poor sanitary risks.

Recommendations

· Plan to have no or little food left over. Leftovers can be wasteful and are a bacteriological hazard.
· In a well managed food-service operation, highly perishable cooked foods are used within the day of their preparation. Check for leftovers after each meal and plan their immediate use.
· Protect food from contamination during storage at all times.
· Daily check refrigerators for sanitary condition, spills, orderliness, and correct temperature.

For handling of specific items, see Part III-F.

Chilling of Displayed Food

. Cold foods to be consumed cold must be kept chilled while displayed. This includes fruit juices and other cold foods that are not hazardous from a public health point of view.

. Examples of menu items that are potentially hazardous and must be constantly kept chilled for the purpose of bacteriological safety are milk, milk drinks, cream, yoghurt and other perishable dairy products; seafood cocktails; canapes; hors d'oeuvres; cold cuts, meat, poultry, sausage, fish, eggs; salads and sandwiches made with proteinaceous ingredients; potato salad; cold platters; custards; puddings; cream fillings and cream-filled pastries, pies, and cakes; meringued pies; and desserts made with milk and/or egg, and many more.

Prevent Multiplication of Bacteria in Frozen Foods

Remember that freezing does not kill bacteria and that bacteria injurious to health may survive freezer storage for months. Also, the survivors will resume multiplication when food has thawed, namely, when ice crystals have melted.

Recommendations for Handling Frozen Food

1. Purchase frozen food from a reputable dealer; check deliveries and refuse items showing signs of defrosting. Do not overstock on frozen food.
2. Move delivered items immediately into a freezer maintained at 0°F or colder. Although a storage temperature of 0°F is satisfactory, the freezer

temperature is apt to rise when the door is opened frequently, and when large amounts of warm food are introduced.

3. In frozen items that can be cooked in the frozen state, the many dangers connected with defrosting are eliminated. When frozen items must be defrosted, they should not be allowed to warm up beyond 45°F.

4. *Defrosting Procedures*
   Fresh Frozen Foods Served Unheated
   Fruit Juice Concentrates: Reconstitute from frozen state and chill at once.
   Fruit: Defrost in original container in the refrigerator, or (in a tightly sealed, moisture-proof container) in cold running water.
   Fresh Frozen Foods to Be Heated
   Fruits: Defrost just enough for convenience in handling; defrost in a refrigerator or in a tightly sealed moisture-proof container in cold running water. Fruit, defrosted at room temperature, tends to turn mushy and discolors.
   Vegetables: Do not defrost, except corn on the cob, spinach, asparagus, and broccoli.
   Fish, Shellfish, Meats (Small Cuts), and Poultry (Small Cuts): Do not defrost unless breaded or covered with batter. If you wish to defrost, place items in the refrigerator. or enclosed in tightly sealed, moisture-proof bags in *cold* running water.
   Large Roasts, Whole Turkeys, or Frozen Egg: Always defrost in the refrigerator. Meat and turkey, if enclosed in tightly sealed, moisture-proof bags, and eggs, may also be defrosted in *cold* running water.
   Precooked Frozen Foods
   The manufacturers' directions will state whether the particular item requires defrosting and how it should be done. Remember that defrosting in the refrigerator is always safer than defrosting at kitchen temperatures.

Management has the obligation to:

1. Set up detailed guidelines (Worksheet) concerning defrosting, which should state:
   What food is to be defrosted.
   When to remove it from the freezer.
   Where it should be defrosted.
   How it should be defrosted.

2. Provide the necessary refrigerator space and equipment.

3. Provide supervision.

The food handler has the obligation to:

1. Follow instructions.

SAMPLE WORKSHEET
Directions for Defrosting Frozen Foods

Description of food	To be defrosted: Yes No	When to be removed from freezer	Place of defrosting	Additional directions and special precautions
Whole turkey 20-23 lb	X	3 days before cooking	Refrigeration (specify which)	Do not remove original wrapper

2. Report to the supervisor, if the instructions do not work well, that defrosting times may be "off" and cooperate with the supervisor in improving directions.

3. Carefully check items that are allowed to defrost at room temperatures; should these thaw ahead of time when they are to be cooked, transfer them to a refrigerator for temporary safe holding.

Techniques for Handling Specific Hazardous Menu Items

In the Tables 8 through 22, recommendations are made for the safe handling, heating, hot-holding, cooling, and cold storage of certain menu items. Precautions in the use of leftovers are also listed.

The menu items selected are those that are frequently mentioned in connection with food-poisoning outbreaks; they are the so-called potentially hazardous items. Their preparation requires the strictest sanitary care at every step.

Table 8. Safety of Creamed Items

Safe Preparation	Safe Heating and Hot-Holding	Safe Refrigeration	Precautions in Use of Leftovers
Use safe, wholesome ingredients; do not use leftovers of doubtful age and wholesomeness.	In general, it is better management and safer to hold sauce and solid ingredients separately until just before serving time; creamed mixtures are a greater risk when held combined than are the sauce and the solids when held separately; also, danger of curdling and of other undesirable changes is lessened.	Creamed foods are hazardous; refrigerate them promptly and quickly.	Heat to at least 165°F before serving; this heat treatment will kill many contaminants except heat-resistant spores, and toxins of staphylococci.
Work with clean hands, cutting boards, knives, and other equipment.		Precool thin mixtures (in original cooking utensil), using cold running water; thick mixtures in shallow pans set in ice; if amounts of leftovers are small (1 gallon), refrigerate without precooling.	It is almost impossible to predict when the food becomes unsafe; its entire history influences keeping quality and safeness.
Work speedily and efficiently; do not expose foods to contaminants and warmth any longer than absolutely necessary.	Creamed foods do not conduct heat well; therefore, have sauce as hot as feasible when adding the solids (meat, egg, seafood, etc.).	Store in the refrigerator in a covered container; use soon, within 24 hours.	Noticeable signs of spoilage (slime, mold, or souring) indicate the presence of microorganisms that may or may not be harmful; it may indicate mishandling and mismanagement.
If ingredients that are to be added to sauce are prepared in advance, refrigerate them until the time for mixing them with the cream sauce has come.	Reheat combined mixture to 165°F or higher.		Absence of spoilage signs does not guarantee safeness.
	Hold mixture above 140°F until ready to serve.		DISCARD SUSPECT ITEMS

Table 9.   Safety of Egg-Thickened Desserts: Stirred Custards, Cream Fillings, Puddings, and Cream-Filled Baked Goods

Safe Preparation	Safe Heating	Safe Refrigeration	Precautions in Use of Leftovers
Use sound-shelled fresh eggs or pasteurized (*Salmonella*-free) processed egg.	Prepare a suspension of one fourth of the cold milk, starch and egg; add slurry to hot milk, and allow to thicken. Mixture is done when raw starch flavor has disappeared.	*Stirred (soft) custards:* precool to 80°F with the aid of cold running water, under agitation. Refrigerate, covered, in 2 to 3 gallon batches.	It is almost impossible to predict accurately when the food becomes unsafe; its entire history influences keeping quality and safeness.
When using shell eggs, prevent pieces of shell from falling into the broken-out egg.		*Fillings and puddings:* precool like custard or refrigerate at once, covered, in shallow pans.	Noticeable spoilage signs (slime, mold, or souring) indicate the presence of microorganisms that may or may not be harmful. They indicate mishandling and mismanagement.
Break each egg into a small dish and inspect for signs of spoilage, as one spoiled egg may ruin an entire batch of eggs; discard suspect eggs.	Whenever feasible, cooked mixtures should be placed in cakes, shells, crusts or other baked goods while still hot (at least 140°F); fillings not to be used immediately following preparation should be refrigerated at once and kept cold.	Mixtures should be at 45°F or colder within 1 hour.	
Prevent contamination of broken-out shell egg, frozen egg, or dried egg; sources of contamination are hands, soiled ladles, and other equipment and utensils.		Cream-filled and custard-filled cakes and pastries must be kept under constant refrigeration.	Absence of spoilage signs does not guarantee safeness. DISCARD SUSPECT ITEMS
Prevent contamination of the cooked product.		Use stirred custards, cream fillings, puddings, and cream-filled baked goods, within 24 hours.	

Table 10. Safety of Meringued Pies

Safe Preparation	Safe Heating	Safe Refrigeration	Precautions in Use of Leftovers
Use sound-shelled fresh eggs or pasteurized (*Salmonella*-free) processed eggs.	Bake in moderate oven (325 to 350°F) for 16 or 20 minutes. Reason: meringues baked quickly at higher temperatures become brown on top before the portion near the filling is done and are not thoroughly heated.	Keep finished pies under constant refrigeration. Use within 24 hours.	It is almost impossible to predict accurately when the food becomes unsafe; its entire history influences keeping quality and safeness.
Prepare crust.			
Prepare filling.			Noticeable spoilage signs (slime, mold, or souring) indicate the presence of microorganisms that may or may not be harmful. They indicate mishandling and mismanagement.
Prepare meringue.			
Pour filling into crusts while filling is still hot (at least 158°F) and add meringue immediately.			
Bake pies while filling is still hot.			Absence of spoilage signs does not guarantee safeness.
			DISCARD SUSPECT ITEMS

Table 11. Safety of Hollandaise

Recommendations

Use high-quality, sound-shelled fresh eggs or pasteurized processed eggs.

Stagger production. Prepare a new batch every two hours. This sauce cannot be held at safe (140°F and higher) temperatures without disintegrating in consistency, therefore prepare only small amounts at a time.

Discard sauce that has been held more than two hours at temperatures below 140°F.

Table 12.   Safety of Menu Items Containing Uncooked Egg

Items	Recommendations
ACID ITEMS Mayonnaise and uncooked salad dressing	Use high-quality sound-shelled eggs, or pasteurized (*Salmonella*-free) processed egg. Prevent contamination of egg mass from pieces of shell, spoiled egg, soiled ladles, soiled hands and other sources. Use clean equipment for preparation and storage of dressing. Store, covered, in the refrigerator. Do not contaminate the dressing when removing portions from the batch. Use clean utensils.
NONACID ITEMS (a) Desserts made with egg foam, such as chiffon-type items and whips	Use high-quality sound-shelled eggs, or pasteurized (*Salmonella*-free) processed egg white. Prevent contamination of egg from pieces of shell, spoiled egg, soiled ladles, soiled hands, and other sources. Use clean bowls and beaters in whipping, folding, and dipping procedures. Refrigerate finished items at once and keep under continuous refrigeration until served. Serve within 24 hours.
(b) Egg-enriched nourishment, such as eggnog.	The use of uncooked shell eggs in nourishment for patients is inadvisable because of the danger from *Salmonella*. Pasteurized processed egg, although rendered free from *Salmonella* in pasteurization, may well become recontaminated. Remember that the very young, the aged, the frail, and the sick are particularly sensitive to *Salmonella*. Commercial eggnog mixes made with pasteurized egg may be used with precaution: the powder must be kept in a closed container and protected from contaminates; and clean spoons must be used to remove the portion to be reconstituted into fluid eggnog. Once reconstituted, eggnog is excellent food for bacteria and therefore must be kept chilled. Eggnog left for hours by the patient's bedside becomes warm and a menace to the patient. Baked custard may be served in place of eggnog if solid nourishment is permitted.

Table 13. Safety of Soups and Soup Base

Safe Preparation	Safe Heating and Hot-Holding	Safe Refrigeration	Precautions in Use of Leftovers
Use safe, wholesome ingredients; beware of using leftovers of doubtful history. Work with clean hands, use clean cutting boards, knives, and other equipment and utensils.	In general, soups made with stock are boiled or brought to a boil; this is effective in destroying contaminants, although heat-resistant spores of *C. perfringens* may survive. Cream soups, especially those containing seafood and leftovers, should be heated to as high a temperature as possible, at least 165°F. Do not prepare large amounts of stock and soup in advance unless you can keep them safe, either hot (140° or above) or cold (45°F or below).	Precool in cooling kettle, using agitation; or precool in 2 to 4 gallon batches, setting stock pots in cold running water and stirring occasionally (every 15 to 30 minutes). When the steaming stops, refrigerate. Avoid contamination from soiled containers, soiled spoons, hands, dust, etc. Store in refrigerator in covered containers. Use leftover soups as soon as possible, preferably within 24 hours.	With prolonged storage, the number of bacteria will increase; toxin of staphylococci may form. Reheat leftover stock and soup to a boil before serving, unless it is served cold. It is almost impossible to predict accurately when the food becomes unsafe. Its entire history influences keeping quality and safeness. Absence of spoilage signs does not guarantee safeness; activities of food-poisoning bacteria do not noticeably change appearance, odor, or flavor of contaminated items. DISCARD SUSPECT ITEMS.

Table 14. Safety of Fish and Shellfish Items: General Directions

Safe Preparation	Safe Heating and Hot-Holding	Safe Refrigeration	Precautions in Use of Leftovers
Use safe, wholesome fish and shellfish harvested from unpolluted waters.	Use certified, safe raw materials only. Some shellfish, like oysters and clams, are eaten uncooked or very lightly heated.	Fish and shellfish are to be kept under constant refrigeration except during actual preparation.	It is almost impossible to predict accurately when the food becomes unsafe; its entire history influences quality and safeness.
If frozen and if it needs to be defrosted, follow approved methods of defrosting (see pages 167-169).	Serve cooked seafood immediately when desired stage of doneness is reached. Holding these items at safe (140°F) temperatures for long may toughen them, while holding them at temperatures below 140°F invites bacterial growth. Therefore, STAGGER PRODUCTION.	Precool leftover cooked seafood by recommended procedures, then refrigerate.

Use leftovers promptly (within 24 hours). | Noticeable spoilage signs (slime, mold, souring, etc.) indicate the presence of microorganisms that may or may not be harmful, but that indicate mishandling and mismanagement. |
Use clean hands, cutting boards, and utensils; use care in deboning, and deveining; wash hands frequently.			Absence of signs of spoilage does not guarantee safeness; activities of food poisoning bacteria do not noticeably change appearance, odor, or flavor.
If items are breaded, use special precautions that prevent the build-up of bacteria in the egg mixture. Prepare fresh mixture each hour.			DISCARD SUSPECT ITEMS.
Manage preparation so that seafood does not remain at lukewarm temperatures longer than 1 hour at the most. Keep items under refrigeration except when actually manipulated.			

Table 15.   Safety of Gravies

Safe Preparation	Safe Heating and Hot-Holding	Safe Refrigeration	Precautions in Use of Leftovers
Prevent contamination of ingredients as well as finished gravy. Use clean equipment and utensils in preparation.	Boil or simmer gravies and reheat them each time after a chance for contamination has occurred; for example:	Refrigerate leftover gravy at once. Precool in cooling kettle or in 1-gallon stock pots set in water or ice; stir occasionally.	Do not add freshly-prepared gravy to leftover gravy. Before serving leftover gravy, reheat thoroughly; boiling or simmering is recommended.
Prevent multiplication of contaminants by keeping the gravy hot or cold.	(a) reheat poultry gravy to simmer, or boil, after adding chopped ingredients such as giblets.	Store the gravy in a covered container; use within 1 to 2 days.	It is almost impossible to predict when the food becomes unsafe; its entire history influences keeping quality and safeness.
	(b) reheat meat gravy to simmer or boil after adding juice from cooked roast.		Noticeable spoilage signs (slime, mold, souring, etc.) indicate the presence of microorganisms and indicate mishandling and mismanagement.
	Keep gravy hot (simmering) until serving time. If prepared in advance, cool quickly and refrigerate.		Absence of spoilage signs does not guarantee safeness. DISCARD SUSPECT ITEMS.

Table 16. Safety of Meat Roasts (Other Than Pork and Ham)

Safe Preparation	Safe Heating and Hot-Holding	Safe Refrigeration	Precautions in Use of Leftovers
Use only meat inspected by the Government for wholesomeness.	Plan roasting time of rolled roast so that the roast is finished just before serving. This is recommended because of the danger from inside contamination during deboning and rolling. A contaminant of special importance is *C. perfringens*; its spores survive roasting.	Before handling meat, wash hands. Use clean sanitized work surfaces, equipment, and utensils. Avoid using hands any more than absolutely necessary.	Avoid contamination and warming of meat whenever it is temporarily removed from refrigeration during storage.
Use separate working surfaces and equipment for raw and cooked meat. If this is not feasible, thoroughly clean and sanitize work tables, chopping blocks, slicers, etc. after they are used for raw meat. (See III-B for techniques.)		Chill cooked meat separately from juice and gravy.	It is almost impossible to predict when the food becomes unsafe; its entire history influences keeping quality and safeness.
Thoroughly wash hands after handling raw meat.	Ideally, the period of hot-holding should not exceed two hours.	Bone-in, cooked roasts may be refrigerated in bulk. Refrigerate promptly.	Noticeable signs of spoilage (slime, mold, souring, etc.) indicate mishandling and mismanagement.
Keep meat cold until ready to be roasted.	Rolled roasts to be served cold should be sliced soon after cooking; place slices in shallow pans no more than 2 to 3″ deep; cover and refrigerate at once.	Boned cooked roasts cool quickly and more safely if sliced. Arrange slices in shallow pans, cover, and chill at once.	Absence of spoilage signs does not guarantee safeness.
Defrost frozen roasts in a refrigerator.		Refrigerate only the amount that can be used in 1 to 3 days; freeze the rest	DISCARD SUSPECT ITEMS.

Table 17.   Safety of Cooked Pork and Ham

Special Hazards	Recommendations
Danger from trichinae.	Roast fresh pork to 170°F. Cook all pork to the gray (done) stage.
Danger from fecal streptococci.	Bake hams to 170°F, including tenderized and fully cooked items.

Table 18. Safety of Poultry Items[a]

Safe Preparation	Safe Heating and Hot-Holding	Safe Refrigeration	Precautions in Use of Leftovers
Use only poultry Government inspected for wholesomeness.	Poultry is not acceptable unless cooked to doneness.	Cool and store meat separately from gravy.	It is almost impossible to predict when the food becomes unsafe; its entire history influences keeping quality and safeness.
Defrost frozen poultry in a refrigerator.	Fortunately, cooking to the well-done stage eliminates the danger of salmonellae	Refrigerate leftovers promptly.	
Keep poultry cold until ready to be prepared.	surviving the cooking. However, stuffed large turkeys are not safe.	Leftover whole turkey should be deboned and meat placed in clean shallow pans or on	Noticeable signs of spoilage (slime, mold, souring, etc.) indicate mishandling and mis-management.
Thoroughly wash inside of poultry carcass before roasting. Wash giblets.	If giblets are used in gravy, chop cooked giblets on sanitized board, add to gravy,	trays. Be sure working surfaces are clean and sanitized. Cover, and refrigerate no	Absence of spoilage signs does not guarantee safeness.
Use separate working surfaces and equipment for raw and cooked poultry. If this is not feasible, thoroughly clean and sanitize work surfaces and equipment that were previously used for raw poultry (see III-B). Only then use them for cooked items.	and boil gravy. Total warm holding of poultry and gravy should not exceed 2 hours.	longer than 1 to 2 days.	DISCARD SUSPECT ITEMS.
Thoroughly wash hands after handling raw poultry.			

[a] See also Table 19, "Safety of Deboned Poultry."

Table 19.   Safety of Deboned Poultry[a]

Safe Preparation	Safe Heating and Hot-Holding	Safe Refrigeration	Precautions in Use of Leftovers
Poultry may be deboned while raw.	Meat is safe when cooked to doneness; the dangers arise from handling the cooked meat and holding it at temperatures at which bacterial growth is possible.	To refrigerate poultry, arrange meat in shallow layers, whether it is the entire bird, large pieces, or chopped meat.	Use cooked poultry the same day, if at all possible.
Cook poultry to doneness.			Menu items made with much-handled poultry meat, such as salads and creamed items (à la king) are frequently the cause of food-poisoning outbreaks.
Move cooked poultry to shallow pans or trays to cool in a cold place away from dust and other chances for contamination.		Cover and refrigerate no longer than 1 to 2 days.	
Unless deboned previously, remove meat from bones as soon as meat is sufficiently cool to handle.			It is almost impossible to predict when the food becomes unsafe; its entire history influences keeping quality and safeness.
Do not allow the process to drag along; the job should be completed in 20 to 30 minutes.			Noticeable signs of spoilage (slime, mold, souring, etc.) indicate mishandling and mismanagement.
Place meat in shallow pans or on trays to cool fast and chop when cool; or chop at once, place meat in shallow pans or on trays and cool.			Absence of spoilage signs do not guarantee safeness. DISCARD SUSPECT ITEMS.

Table 19. (Continued)

Safe Preparation	Safe Heating and Hot-Holding	Safe Refrigeration	Precautions in Use of Leftovers
Work with meticulously clean hands. Wash hands before starting work and each time you touch anything other than the meat.			
Use clean and sanitized chopping board. If possible, use board not previously used for raw meat.			

[a] Prepared for use in creamed dishes, salads, sandwiches, and other combination dishes. See also Table 8, "Safety of Creamed Items"; Table 20, "Safety of Salads"; Table 21, "Safety of Sandwiches"; and Table 22, "Safety of Hot Menu Items."

Table 20. Safety of Salads (Potato, Meat, Poultry, Egg, and Seafood)

Safe Preparation	Safe Heating and Hot-Holding	Safe Refrigeration	Precautions in Use of Leftovers
Use safe, wholesome ingredients; especially beware of leftovers of doubtful history or old leftovers.	No heat can be applied to the ingredients or the finished salads.	Keep hazardous ingredients and salads chilled at all times except during actual preparation.	Potato, meat, poultry, egg and seafood salads have been indicted many times in outbreaks of food-borne illness.
Have the ingredients cold.		Heat transfer is slow in salads; thus, cooling in large batches represents a special hazard. Do not pile salad high in a large container; cool in shallow (3″) pans to speed heat transfer; cover salads.	Leftover salads exposed to warm temperature several hours before refrigeration are hazardous, as are salads repeatedly removed from refrigerator and exposed to warm temperatures.
Work with clean hands and equipment when preparing ingredients and combining them.			
Add acid ingredients to main ingredients at early stage of preparation.		Use as soon as possible, certainly within 24 hours.	It is almost impossible to predict when the food becomes suspect; its entire history influences keeping quality and safeness.
Use about ⅓ of the salad dressing (use it in the form marinade) immediately after the potatoes, meat, poultry or seafood have been peeled, sliced, chopped, deboned, etc.; the more acid dressing is used, the greater is its inhibitory effect on the bacteria. Refrigerate marinated mixture and add remaining ingredients just before serving.			Noticeable signs of spoilage (slime, mold, souring, etc.) indicate mishandling and mismanagement.
			Absence of spoilage signs does not guarantee safeness.
			DISCARD SUSPECT ITEMS.

Safe Preparation	Safe Heating and Hot-Holding	Safe Refrigeration	Precautions in Use of Leftovers
Use safe, wholesome ingredients; beware of leftovers of doubtful history.	Hot sandwiches should be thoroughly heated, or made with thoroughly heated ingredients (meat, gravy, etc.) and served at once.	Do not stack high; spread them in shallow layers on trays to a height of 3 to 4."	Sandwiches that contain hazardous ingredients and are exposed to warm temperatures for hours are suspect. DISCARD.
Prepare sandwiches from chilled ingredients, except butter.	Heat cannot be applied to cold sandwiches.	Keep under strict refrigeration at all times; this includes display area on cafeteria counters.	
Work with clean hands and equipment.		Use within 24 hours.	
Wrap sandwiches for display.			
Stagger production; place finished sandwiches on shallow trays no more than approximately 3 to 4" high; refrigerate. Start a new batch frequently.			
If feasible, use acid to discourage bacterial multiplication; place pickle, salad dressing, mayonnaise, prepared mustard, horseradish, etc. next to meat or other hazardous fillings.			
Chill finished sandwiches rapidly; keep chilled until served.			
On catered, wrapped sandwiches, show the date of preparation.			

Table 22.　Safety of Hot Menu Items Made With Ground, Minced, Chopped, Flaked, Cubed, or Otherwise Comminuted Meat, Poultry, Egg, Fish, and Shellfish

Safe Preparation	Safe Heating and Hot-Holding	Safe Refrigeration	Precautions in Use of Leftovers
Use fresh, wholesome ingredients. Beware of leftovers.	*Group I (meat, poultry and seafood patties, cakes, croquettes and hamburgers* cooked to the medium rare or rare stage):	Plan production of these hazardous items in such a way that there are few or no leftovers.	Leftovers *of items made with fresh ingredients:*
If leftovers must be used, take only those that were treated in a sanitary manner, chilled rapidly, and refrigerator-stored for no longer than 24 hours.	Keep items under refrigeration until heated.	Leftovers of menu items in which leftovers have been used are particularly hazardous. DO NOT REUSE.	Use within 24 hours. DISCARD SUSPECT ITEMS.
Work with clean hands; use clean work surfaces, equipment, and utensils.	Stagger the heating in such a way that each batch is consumed within one half hour of having finished cooking, or sooner. Warm holding for extended periods is hazardous.		Leftovers *of items made with leftover ingredients:* DISCARD.
Work rapidly. Unless items are cooked at once, place them in a refrigerator and bring them out as needed.	*Group II (casseroles and meat and poultry pies):*		
Treat with respect all egg mixtures used in breading and battering. Make up fresh mixture every hour or so to prevent build-up of food-poisoning bacteria that may stem from the meat, the worker's hands, soiled equipment, or all of these.	Keep items under refrigeration until heated.		
	For thorough heating, cook in moderate oven until the mixture boils. *Do not* heat under the broiler.		
	Group III (turkey stuffing): Bake separately from turkey		

Important Facts in Brief for Part III

- Sanitation of the physical plant involves:
  1. Cleanability of walls, floors, and ceiling.
  2. Proper sewage disposal and plumbing; presence of floor drains where required because of spillage or method of cleaning floor.
  3. Good ventilation.
  4. Good lighting.
  5. Adequate hand-washing facilities.
  6. Sanitary dressing rooms or locker room and sanitary toilet facilities.
  7. Sanitary garbage disposal.
  8. Control of rodents and insects.
  9. Separate storage area for cleaning materials and utensils.
  10. Regular and adequate cleaning of the facility.

- The primary objective of any cleaning operation is to remove soil and control bacteria. This is necessary to prevent food spoilage, reduce health hazards, and control odors.
- The main cleaning agent is water. Detergents and friction help water do a better job.
- Clean water at 170°F for one minute is necessary to rinse away soil and sanitize the item being cleaned.
- To plan a successful cleaning operation, the cleaner must consider the nature of the water, the type of soil, the corrosion resistance of the material being cleaned, the type of cleaner, and the condition of the soil.
- Cutting, dicing, and mixing equipment should be easy to dismantle so parts that come in contact with food can be properly cleaned and sanitized.
- The sanitary concern of primary equipment such as ovens, fryers, and broilers is one of odor control, aesthetics, and equipment efficiency.
- Dishwashing or pot-and-pan machines require regular cleaning if dishes and utensils are to be properly cleaned and sanitized.
- Transportation and dish-storage equipment needs to be cleaned regularly to avoid recontamination of clean dishes and pans.

• A written cleaning procedure is a useful training tool and serves as a standard for judging the quality of performance.

• A checklist provides a handy reference of items that need to be cleaned and the frequency of cleaning required.

• For a sanitation program to be effective, one should start with a sound food supply. To assure wholesomeness, it is of greatest importance to specify exactly what one wants.

• Some foods must be considered potentially hazardous because of their composition and/or the handling they receive. The definition of hazardous foods as given by the U. S. Public Health Service reads as follows:

"Potentially Hazardous Food shall mean any perishable food which consists in whole or in part of milk or milk products, eggs, meat, poultry, fish, shellfish, or other ingredients, capable of supporting rapid and progressive growth of infectious or toxigenic microorganisms."

• The health of the food handler plays an important part in sanitation. Food handlers can be sources of bacteria causing illness through transmission of disease germs or through food poisoning.

• Management and employees should cooperate in the effort to keep ill employees from working with food, and with equipment and utensils used in preparing and serving food.

• To safeguard the wholesomeness of finished menu items at the time they are served, the following rules need to be observed:

1. Start out with wholesome food material.
2. Remove dirt, soil, and chemical residues by washing thoroughly.
3. Protect food from contamination with poisonous substances, soil, and disease-producing bacteria throughout its preparation, storage, and service.
4. Thoroughly heat those foods that can be expected to harbor illness-producing microorganisms whenever feasible.
5. Prevent multiplication of microorganisms in the food and on equipment used in food preparation, storage, and service.

Study Questions for Part III

1. What is the food operator's responsibility to his customer?
2. What is the primary objective of any cleaning operation? Why is this objective necessary?
3. What is the main cleaning agent? What functions do detergents and friction serve?
4. Under what conditions is water a satisfactory sanitizer?
5. What features are important in purchasing food-preparation equipment?
6. Why are chopping, grinding, and mixing machines considered to have a high potential for causing microbial contamination of food?
7. What information should a cleaning schedule give?
8. What government agencies are responsible for safeguarding the wholesomeness of food?
9. What food products are considered potentially hazardous?
10. What is meant by the "danger zone" in food handling?
11. What time-temperature relationships must be observed in order to pasteurize milk?
12. What are the general rules for purchasing a sound food supply?
13. What are the general rules for checking deliveries and storage of food?
14. What are management's responsibilities in "safe" food handling? What are the employee's responsibilities?

Readings for Part III

Bjornson, B. F. "Control of Domestic Rats and Mice". U.S. Department of Health, Education and Welfare, Public Health Service. PHS Publ. No. 563. 1960.

Blaker, Gertrude G. "Good Sanitation Technics" *School Lunch* 17(3):74. 1963.

Clawson, Augusta H. *Equipment Maintenance Manual.* Ahrens Publishing Company, Inc. New York 1951.

Entomology Research Division, Agricultural Research Service. "Cockroaches—How to Control Them". USDA Leaflet No. 430, revised. 1962.

Hobart Manufacturing Company, Troy, Ohio. "Instruction Manuals for Flite Dishwasher and Vertical Food Chopper."

Hobbs, Betty. *Food Poisoning and Food Hygiene.* 2nd ed. Edward Arnold, Ltd., London. 1968. Part II-10.

Kotschevar, Lendal H. and Margaret Terrell. *Food Service Planning*: Layout and Equipment. John Wiley and Sons, New York. 1961. Sections II-9, III.

Kotschevar, Lendal H. *Quantity Food Purchasing.* John Wiley and Sons, Inc. New York. 1961.

Longrée, Karla. *Quantity Food Sanitation.* 2nd ed. Wiley-Interscience, a division of John Wiley and Sons, New York. 1972. Chapters VIII, IX, X, XI, XII, XIII.

Stauffer, Lee D. "Sanitation in Hospital Food Service." Reprints to be obtained from *Hospitals,* Journal of the American Hospital Association, July 16, August 1, August 16, September 1, September 16. 1964.

Tressler, D. K., B. W. Van Arsdel, and M. J. Copley. *The Freezing Preservation of Foods.* 4th ed. Avi Publishing Co., Westport, Conn. 1968. Vol. 4, Chapters 24 and 25.

U.S. Department of Health, Education and Welfare, Public Health Service. *Food Service Sanitation Manual.* PHS Publ. No. 934, Washington, D. C. 1962.

U.S. Department of Health, Education and Welfare, Public Health Service. *The Vending of Food and Beverages.* A Sanitation Ordinance and Code. PHS Publ. No. 546, Washington, D. C. 1965.

West, B. B., Levelle Wood, and Virginia Harger. *Food Service in Institutions,* 4th ed. John Wiley and Sons, New York. 1965. Sections I-3 and II-9; III-10 and III-11.

PART IV

Education and Training in Sanitation of Food-Service Personnel

People can make or break a good sanitation program. The important role that workers and management play in the safe handling of food has been stressed throughout this book. The money, time, and effort that go into a sanitation program are wasted if the people working in food service are not aware of or knowledgeable about appropriate sanitary practices.

Sanitation-conscious workers don't just happen. They are developed by providing good leadership, the proper tools to do the job, and continuous training and follow-up to develop safe food-handling habits. Supervision or follow-up of recommended sanitation procedures must be carried out daily if the worker is to believe that sanitation is important.

Industrial training may be defined as the art of helping an employee to acquire "desirable habits" necessary for the performance of his task. Habits result from practice or repetitive doing. Desirable habits result from the practice of the correct procedures; thus, before the new employee can start practicing, he must have a clear mental picture of what he is trying to accomplish and know why this is important. By the same token, the trainer must also have a clear mental picture of what he wants done and how the job should be accomplished.

Before developing a successful sanitation training program, management needs to evaluate the current sanitation procedures in use. There is little point in expending resources on any training programs if that training results in ineffective sanitation procedures. Top management must be willing to provide the necessary people, tools, and equipment to implement effective sanitation on a continuing basis. A common and justifiable complaint from the worker is that he is frequently required to attend training sessions and then is not able to apply what he has learned to his job because of the lack of time, money, materials, or equipment.

The teaching ability and work habits of the potential trainers should also be evaluated. Management should not assume that because a supervisor knows how to do a job, he therefore does that job in the most effective manner or can teach others to do the job properly. The frequency with which food-service establishments are cited as being unsanitary would suggest that it is easier to teach the "wrong way" to do a job than the "right way." Too often this is due to the instructor. Usually the trainer teaches the worker to do the job in the same order in which he, the instructor, does it. This may not be the best sequence for the beginner, thus the trainer may confuse rather than teach the worker. Almost always the trainer thinks of the cleaning job in bigger units than the new worker can understand. Hence the instructor overlooks many of the small but essential details the worker must learn in order to do the job successfully. Unless the trainer is freed of his other responsibilities during the training period, he may not have time to teach the whole job at one time. When training is done in "bits and pieces," the learner never gets a clear mental picture of the total job or the explanation of why the job must be done a certain way. As a result the worker is tempted to develop shortcuts which lead to unsatisfactory cleaning practices. Even more important, if the teacher does not have time to do constructive follow-up of the training, the student may develop undesirable work habits relative to sanitation. Thus the first step in developing a good training program may well be to train the trainer.

The J.I.T.* technique developed by the government during World War II has been used successfully in training. This technique is divided into two parts. The first part gives the key activities of the trainer that are necessary before training starts. The second part gives the four basic steps required in training the worker.

Before training can start, the trainer should develop a training plan and schedule. The training plan answers the question of *who* is going to be trained, *what,* and *where.* The training schedule tells *when* training will be done. Next the trainer should prepare a written job breakdown of the cleaning activity to be accomplished. This job breakdown or cleaning procedure will list the important steps in the activity and the key points necessary for accomplishing each step. Such a cleaning procedure can serve as a teaching tool during the period of instruction, as a reference point for the student during his practice session, as the instructor's check sheet during the follow-up, and as an evaluation tool in checking results. Finally, the trainer will need to get ready to teach by securing the necessary supplies and equipment for the job. The work place must be arranged as it will appear when the worker is responsible for the cleaning. The trainee should be able to stand next to rather than across from the instructor during the demonstration. It is very important that the trainee stand in approximately the same position as he will when he is actually doing the job. If he stands

* Job Industry Training.

across from the instructor he will get a mirror image rather than a true image of the procedure. This may result in confusion when he takes his position in front of the equipment in the practice session.

The four basic steps in training can be outlined as follows:

1. Prepare the employee for instruction.
   (a) Put the worker at ease.
   (b) Create in the student a desire to learn the specific task by explaining the job.
   (c) Stress:
       1. The importance of good sanitation relative to this job.
       2. Safety.
       3. Operational efficiency.
2. Present the job.
   (a) Set a clear pattern for the learner to follow by using the cleaning procedure.
   (b) Explain and demonstrate one step at a time.
   (c) Stress the key points.
   (d) Discuss and show the minor details that are necessary to accomplish the job.
   (e) Omit all material that is not important for the job.
3. Practice period.
   (a) Have the student do the job.
   (b) Have the student tell and show what he is going to do and why he is doing it.
   (c) Correct errors and omissions as the student makes them.
   (d) Continue to practice until the student is able to give back to the teacher everything that the teacher gave the learner in step 2.
4. Follow through or test.
   (a) Put the worker on his own.
   (b) Encourage questions.
   (c) Come back to the work place frequently to check progress or problems.
   (d) Tell the worker how he's doing.

The instructor must have a clear picture of every detail in his mind; otherwise, he cannot expect to pass that picture on to the student. The instructor must also have skill in handling the equipment, if the learner is to have any confidence in him. The J.I.T. motto is: If the pupil hasn't learned, the teacher hasn't taught. Worker performance, then, is the criterion used to determine the quality of the instruction.

Readings for Part IV

1. Blaker, G. "Good Sanitation Technics." *School Lunch* 17(3):74. 1963.
2. Fischback, H. S. "Sanitation is a part of Menu Planning." *Volume Feeding Management* 61(1):171. 1961.
3. Longrée, Karla. *Quantity Food Sanitation.* 2nd ed. Wiley-Interscience, a division of John Wiley and Sons. New York. 1972. Chapter XIV.
4. Standard Brands, Inc., "How to Train—Job Instructors Guide, Tested Management Techniques." Standard Brands, Inc., New York, New York.
5. Stauffer, Lee D. "From Pots and Pans to Large Appliances: Equipment and Food Safety." In *Sanitation in Hospital Food Service,* reprinted from *Hospitals,* Journal of the American Hospital Association, August 16, 1964.
6. U. S. Printing Office. *Food Service Sanitation Manual.* Public Health Service Publication No. 934. 1962.

Visual Aids

Package FS-1 Hospital Food Service Series—Sanitation.
Five film strips and records that accompany the film strips.
Trainex Corporation, P.O. Box 116, Garden Grove, California. 92642
"Protecting the Public" tells your employees:
Part one—the personal side.
Part two—food protection.
Part three—establishment and equipment sanitation.
The Educational Materials Center, National Restaurant Association, 1530 N. Lake Shore Drive, Chicago, Illinois 60610.

Appendix

Table I.   Transmission of Microorganisms Causing Human Respiratory Diseases

Disease	Brief Description of Disease	Organisms Causing Disease	How Disease Is Transmitted from Person to Person	Other Common Routes of Transmission (Indirectly from Person to Person)	How Pathogens Are Transmitted to Food and Then Customers	How to Prevent Transmission of Disease in the Food-Service Department
Common Cold	Sniffles, cough, sinus infection, bronchial infection.	Viruses and bacteria	Germ-laden droplets expelled through sneezing or coughing; discharges from nose and throat; touching with hands soiled by sneezing or coughing or by handling soiled handkerchiefs.	Articles touched, coughed at or sneezed at by a sick person; these articles include food, work surfaces, and utensils used in food preparation and serving.	Through sick or carrier food handlers who prepare and serve food or who handle eating utensils, pots and pans. Through sick or carrier customers who contaminate displayed food or whose eating utensils are not properly sanitized.	Food handlers ill with a cold must not prepare and serve food or handle pots, pans, or eating utensils. Food handlers must cover the mouth when coughing or sneezing, and then wash hands thoroughly. Displayed food must not be touched by customers or exposed to their sneezes or cough droplets. Effective dishwashing must always be practiced.

Table I. (Continued)

Disease	Brief Description of Disease	Organisms Causing Disease	How Disease Is Transmitted from Person to Person	Other Common Routes of Transmission (Indirectly from Person to Person)	How Pathogens Are Transmitted to Food and Then Customers	How to Prevent Transmission of Disease in the Food-Service Department
Septic Sore Throat	Sore throat, fever, body aches, swelling of lymph glands. A person recovered from illness may become a carrier.	Streptococci (hemolytic bacteria).	Most common: germ-laden droplets expelled from throat; soiled hands.	Soiled handkerchiefs and other articles soiled with discharges from the mouth. Food and dishes contaminated with sputum.	Through sick or carrier food handlers who contaminate food and other kitchen objects with discharge from nose and throat. Contaminated eating utensils.	Sick food handlers or carriers must not prepare or serve food nor handle food preparation equipment or eating utensils. Before the patient returns to work, a check should be made by physician to make sure that the patient has not become a carrier. Sanitary dishwashing must always be practiced.
Scarlet Fever (Often Epidemic)	A highly contagious communicable disease that starts with sore throat, fever, and a skin rash. Carriers are possible.	Streptococci (hemolytic bacteria).	Contact with diseased persons and those recuperating. Strict isolation is required in many states for 3 weeks.	All articles that have had contact with disease and convalescent persons, including food and clothing.	Through sick or convalescing food handlers, and "healthy" carriers. Contaminated eating utensils.	(See Septic Sore Throat)

Table I. (Continued)

Disease	Brief Description of Disease	Organisms Causing Disease	How Disease Is Transmitted from Person to Person	Other Common Routes of Transmission (Indirectly from Person to Person)	How Pathogens Are Transmitted to Food and Then Customers	How to Prevent Transmission of Disease in the Food-Service Department
Infection of Tonsils and Adenoids	Fever, sore larynx, cough, sometimes inflammation of eyes, bronchia, and lungs	Viruses	Coughing		(See Septic Sore Throat)	
Pneumonia	Inflammation of the lungs	*Diplococcus pneumoniae,* a bacterium	Droplet infection from a diseased person or carrier.	Hands contaminated with saliva; bacteria can be transmitted through food contaminated through coughing or from contact with contaminated hands.	Through sick or carrier food handlers who contaminate food and other kitchen objects with discharge from nose and throat. Contaminated eating utensils.	Sick food handlers or carriers must not prepare or serve food nor handle food preparation equipment or eating utensils. Before the patient returns to work, a check should be made by physician to make sure that the patient has not become a carrier. Sanitary dishwashing must always be practiced.

Table I.   (Continued)

Disease	Brief Description of Disease	Organisms Causing Disease	How Disease Is Transmitted from Person to Person	Other Common Routes of Transmission (Indirectly from Person to Person)	How Pathogens Are Transmitted to Food and Then Customers	How to Prevent Transmission of Disease in the Food-Service Department
Trench Mouth	Foul-smelling sores in the mouth and throat; also bleeding; raw gums; difficulty in swallowing.	Bacteria	When people are herded together, as soldiers sometimes are, the disease is spread from person to person.	Through food and soiled cups, glasses, and tableware.	Transmission from a sick food handler is possible.	No food handler sick with trench mouth should be allowed to work in the food-service establishment. High sanitary standards of dishwashing are required to kill bacteria left on eating utensils.
Tuberculosis of the Lungs (Pulmonary)	Chest pains, coughing, fever, fatigue, loss of weight. Through X ray of chest, pulmonary tuberculosis can be detected. Bacteria are discharged for a long time by the recuperating patient.	*Mycobacterium tuberculosis,* a bacterium	Most often by droplet infection (coughing); or by fingers soiled with saliva; or by sputum discharged from lungs; or by feces and urine.	Articles soiled with discharge from mouth; or soiled with feces or urine.	Through a sick food handler. Contaminated eating utensils.	Food handlers with tuberculosis must not be allowed to work in a food-service establishment. Sanitary dishwashing must always be practiced.

Table I. *(Continued)*

Disease	Brief Description of Disease	Organisms Causing Disease	How Disease Is Transmitted from Person to Person	Other Common Routes of Transmission (Indirectly from Person to Person)	How Pathogens Are Transmitted to Food and Then Customers	How to Prevent Transmission of Disease in the Food-Service Department
Diphtheria (rare today because of immunization)	At first sore throat and fever. A choking membranelike structure forms in the throat which may extend deeply and suffocate the patient; a powerful toxin poisons the victim's vital organs. Carriers are common.	*Corynebacterium diphtheriae,* a bacterium	Discharge from mouth, throat, and nose.	Articles soiled with discharge from mouth, throat, and nose; contaminated food and eating utensils.	Through sick and carrier food handlers who prepare food or handle eating utensils, pots and pans. Contaminated eating utensils.	Sick food handlers or carriers must not prepare and serve food or handle pots, pans, utensils, dishes, glasses, and flatware. Before the person returns to work, a physician should certify that he is not a carrier. Sanitary dishwashing must always be practiced.
Influenza (Epidemic); also Called "Flu"	Fever, head cold, pharyngitis and other respiratory infections; also, headache, sore throat, muscle pain, weakness.	Viruses	Direct contact; also droplet infection.	Articles soiled with discharge from mouth and nose of sick person; contaminated food and eating utensils.	Through sick food handlers who prepare food or handle eating utensils, pots and pans. Contaminated eating utensils.	Sick food handlers must not prepare and serve food while ill or handle pots, pans, utensils, dishes, glasses, or flatware. Sanitary dishwashing must always be practiced.

Disease	Brief Description Of Disease	Organisms Causing Disease	How Disease Is Transmitted Directly from Person to Person	Other Common Routes of Transmission	How Pathogens Are Transmitted to Food and Then Customers	How Disease Transmission Can Be Prevented in the Food-Service Department
Typhoid Fever	Infection of intestinal tract, continued fever, headache, abdominal pain. Paratyphoid fever is less violent. Carriers are common.	*Salmonella typhi,* a bacterium	By touch, from hands contaminated with the excreta of a diseased person or a carrier.	Through: 1. food handled by a person who is acutely ill or a carrier; this may happen in a kitchen or dairy. 2. Sewage-polluted water. 3. Shellfish harvested from sewage-polluted water and eaten raw. 4. Food visited by flies and other vermin.	Usually through hands of food handler who is or has been ill with typhoid, and is a "healthy" carrier; through drinking sewage-polluted water or eating sewage-polluted food; through contact with vermin such as rodents and flies.	Persons who are ill or carriers must not be allowed in the food preparation and service area and must not touch pots, pans, dishes, glasses, or flatware. Use pure water. Use nonleaky sewer pipes and proper sewage disposal. Use pasteurized milk and other dairy products. Use shellfish from unpolluted water. Practice fly and rodent control.
Bacillary Dysentery (Shigellosis)	A very common illness; diarrhea caused by bacteria (there is another type caused by amebae).	Several species of *Shigella,* a bacterium	By touch and from clothing soiled with excreta of a person who is ill, or a carrier.	Contaminated food; contaminated water; contaminated flies.	Hands of food handler, ill or carrier; leaky sewer pipes.	Persons who are ill or carriers must not be allowed in the food preparation and service area, and must not touch pots, pans, dishes, glasses, or flatware.

Table II. (Continued)

Disease	Brief Description Of Disease	Organisms Causing Disease	How Disease Is Transmitted Directly from Person to Person	Other Common Routes of Transmission	How Pathogens Are Transmitted to Food and and Customers	How Disease Transmission Can Be Prevented in the Food-Service Department
	Carriers are common.					Use pure water. Use nonleaky sewer pipes and proper sewage disposal. Practice fly and rodent control.
Amebic Dysentery	Symptoms are more or less mild and range from mere abdominal discomfort to slight diarrhea alternating with constipation to severe diarrhea. Carriers are common. A person is likely to remain a carrier for life.	Entameba-histolytica, a protozoa	By touch from hands soiled with excreta of contaminated person and by swallowing these contaminants. Many carriers are symptomless.	Contaminated food and water; contaminated flies and rodents, especially rats.	Food and drink handled by diseased persons, convalescents and carriers; sewage-polluted water supply (cross-contamination in plumbing); contaminated flies and rodents that feed on unprotected food items.	Persons who are ill, or carriers, must not handle food or utensils used in the preparation and service of food. Use pure water. Control vermin. Use proper sewage control.

Disease	Brief Description Of Disease	Organisms Causing Disease	How Disease Is Transmitted Directly from Person to Person	Other Common Routes of Transmission	How Pathogens Are Transmitted to Food and and Customers	How Disease Transmission Can Be Prevented in the Food-Service Department
Asiatic Cholera	Rare in the Western world. Intestinal pain and diarrhea, vomiting. Usually fatal. Healthy carriers are not common.	*Vibrio comma*, a bacterium	By touch from hands soiled with excreta of contaminated person and by swallowing the contaminants.	Contaminated food and water; contaminated flies and rodents, especially rats.	Food and drink handled by ill persons; food items exposed to flies and rodents.	See Amebic Dysentery.
Infectious Hepatitis	Infection of the liver. First, fever, nausea, weakness, abdominal pain; then jaundice. Carriers are common.	Viruses		Sewage-contaminated drinking water; sewage-polluted shellfish; food contaminated with excreta of food handler; food contaminated from leaky sewer pipes or other faulty plumbing; flies.	Drinking water supply contaminated through faulty plumbing; use of shellfish harvested from sewage-polluted waters; preparation of food by ill or carrier food handler; faulty plumbing; poor fly control.	Use uncontaminated water supply; purchase and use shellfish from approved sources. Keep toilets in excellent order. Prevent persons ill with hepatitis and carriers from working in food preparation and service. Practice fly control. Keep plumbing in excellent order. Prevent sewage from dripping on food or food-preparation surfaces.

Table III.   Transmission of Germs Causing Diseases in Animals and Humans

Disease	Brief Description of Disease in Man	Organisms Causing Disease	How Disease Is Usually Transmitted to Man	How Pathogens Are Transmitted to Food and Customers	How to Prevent Transmission
Brucellosis A disease of cows; can cause disease in man. (In the human, brucellosis is also called Malta fever or undulant fever.)	Causes irregular fever, sweating, headache, sore throat, pain in joints and muscles.	*Brucella abortus,* a bacterium	Consumption of unpasteurized milk from infected cows.	Use of unpasteurized milk from infected cows.	Use only pasteurized milk.
Tularemia A disease of wild rabbits, squirrels, non edible rodents, and birds. May be transmitted to man.	Causes fever, headache, vomiting, chills, abcess at point of infection.	*Pasteurella tularensis,* a bacterium	Skinning or otherwise handling diseased animals; bite of a tick that had inhabited an infected animal; eating improperly cooked wild rabbit and squirrel.	Use of diseased meat from rabbits, or squirrels, especially when undercooked.	Do not prepare wild rabbit or squirrel for public consumption.

Table III.   (Continued)

Disease	Brief Description of Disease in Man	Organisms Causing Disease	How Disease Is Usually Transmitted to Man	How Pathogens Are Transmitted to Food and Customers	How to Prevent Transmission
Trichinosis A disease of hogs, rabbits, and bears caused by a nematode worm. Disease is spread by feeding hogs infested, uncooked garbage. Other host animals whose meat might serve as human food are rabbits and bears. Trichinae cause disease in man when infested, undercooked meat is eaten.	First symptoms resemble food poisoning (nausea, vomiting, diarrhea, colic). Later-on, muscular soreness and swelling. Death may ensue in severe infestation.	*Trichinella spiralis*, a nematode	Consumption of undercooked, infested meat and sausage. In the U.S.A. incidences of trichinosis in hogs are declining steadily; so are incidences of trichinosis in man.	The larvae of the trichinae are already in the infested meat when cooked; when such meat is undercooked and trichinae are eaten, these are released in the intestinal tract of the human. May propagate in the human and finally settle in the muscle tissues.	Purchase and serve inspected pork and pork products. Serve all pork (including sausage) well done. Roasts should reach a center temperature of at least 165°F, preferably 170°F in the center of the cut. Safe end point is reached when the meat has turned from pink to gray. Cook all small cuts and sausage to the gray stage.

Table IV. Botulism

Illness and Incidence	Brief Description of Illness	Cause and Main Source of Organisms Involved	Growth Requirements, Heat Resistance of Organism	Food Items Frequently Accused of Causing Illness	Circumstances Often Associated with Outbreaks	Principles of Control
Botulinum Food Poisoning (Botulism) Incidence: Infrequent	Fatality high, 65% of cases. Symptoms appear approximately 12 to 36 hours following consumption of the contaminated food; digestive disturbances; nausea; vomiting; diarrhea; dizziness; dryness of throat; double vision; difficulty in swallowing and speaking, followed by in-	Toxin of *Clostridium botulinum,* a spore former. Types A, B and E of importance in U.S.A. Source of organism: soil, for Type A and B; for Type E, sediment of lakes, rivers, and oceans.	Growth and toxin production without air (anaerobically) and at a wide range of temperatures—for growth temperatures Type A and B: 50 to 118°F; Type E: 38 to 113°F. Heat resistance: *spores* are killed when foods are processed by proper methods of heating.	Canned foods of low acidity that have been underprocessed, usually home-canned. Damaged, leaky, rusty cans; cans or jars with broken seals. Contents may or may not have a spoiled appearance. Smoked products that were underprocessed (not heated sufficiently to destroy the spores)	Eating, or merely tasting, suspect items.	*Canned foods:* Use commercially canned foods when preparing food for the public. Refuse donations of home-canned goods. Store canned foods in cool room. Practice quick turnover of canned foods. Do not keep cans long. A year is the longest acceptable period for storing canned foods. Inspect canned goods closely before opening bulging, damaged, rusty, and leaky cans. Contents are suspect if

Table IV. (*Continued*)

Illness and Incidence	Brief Description of Illness	Cause and Main Source of Organisms Involved	Growth Requirements, Heat Resistance of Organism	Food Items Frequently Accused of Causing Illness	Circumstances Often Associated with Outbreaks	Principles of Control
	creasing paralysis of involuntary muscles. Victim dies of inability to breathe.		*Toxins* in canned foods can be destroyed by boiling the food for 15 minutes.	and then held above 38°F.		they spurt out on opening the can, look bubbly, or are off-odor or off-color. *Do not taste suspect food, for it may kill you.* Toxin, if present, is destroyed by boiling the food for 15 minutes. DO NOT EVER TASTE SUSPECT FOOD: Boil for 15 minutes and DISCARD. *Smoked fish:* Keep smoked fish frozen or under strict refrigeration, 38°F or below. Use smoked fish within a few days of refrigerator storage.

Table V.   Staphylococcus Food Poisoning

Illness and Incidence	Brief Description of Illness	Cause and Main Source of Organisms Involved	Growth Requirements, Heat Resistance of Organism	Food Items Frequently Accused of Causing Illness	Circumstances Often Associated with Outbreaks	Principles of Control
Staphylococcus Food Poisoning Incidence: very frequent	Symptoms usually appear 2 to 3 hours (up to 6 hours) after consuming the contaminated item. They are nausea, vomiting, diarrhea, abdominal cramps, all more or less violent; headaches, sweating, weakness. Fatal cases are rare, but may occur when victims are very young, very old, feeble, or ill.	Toxin of *Staphylococcus aureus* *Source* The healthy human body, especially the respiratory tract. Particularly rich in food-poisoning staph is the infected respiratory tract; infected cuts, burns and other wounds; infected ears and eyes; and pimples and boils.	*Growth and toxin production:* Growth occurs between 44 and 114°F. Excellent growth between 70 and 100°F. Staph are salt-loving bacteria. *Heat resistance:* Heating to 165°F kills most of the bacteria themselves, but *not* the toxin. *Toxin* is resistant to heating.	Protein foods, especially those that have undergone much handling (as in chopping, slicing, shaping, or deboning); foods that have been exposed to lukewarm temperatures for more than a couple of hours; and foods that are insufficiently refrigerated because of large bulk or high refrigerator temperature; leftovers in general.	Food handler who was ill with respiratory disease; skin, eye or ear infection. Healthy food handler who failed to practice good personal hygiene, including frequent, thorough washing of hands. Food that was exposed to contaminated hands or equipment. Food that was	Persons suffering from colds, influenza, sore throat, sinus infections, and pus-containing sores should not handle food. All food handlers must be clean. They must not cough or sneeze onto food and must wash their hands after sneezing or coughing. Hands must be washed frequently during preparation of food: after touching likely sources of staph (the person's own body, and other contaminated items such as handkerchiefs).

Table V. *(Continued)*

Illness and Incidence	*Brief Description of Illness*	*Cause and Main Source of Organisms Involved*	*Growth Requirements, Heat Resistance of Organism*	*Food Items Frequently Accused of Causing Illness*	*Circumstances Often Associated with Outbreaks*	*Principles of Control*
		From all these sources staph may contaminate workers' hands and food-preparation equipment. The organism survives fairly long in dust, on walls, on equipment, and on other surfaces.		eral. *Examples:* cream-filled pastries, poultry and meat pies, sandwiches with egg or meat fillings, casseroles and croquettes made with leftovers, chicken salad, potato salad, creamed items, and many others too numerous to mention.	exposed to warm temperatures for long hours. Leftovers were mishandled.	Utensils rather than hands should be used to pick up and manipulate food. Food should be kept hot (140°F or above) or cold (45°F or below). Warm food should be cooled rapidly to safe temperatures.

Table VI. Salmonella Food Infection (Salmonellosis)

Illness and Incidence	Brief Description of Illness	Cause and Main Source of Organisms Involved	Growth Requirements, Heat Resistance of Organism	Food Items Frequently Accused of Causing Illness	Circumstances Often Associated with Outbreaks	Principles of Control
Salmonella Food Infection (Salmonellosis) Incidence: very frequent	Symptoms appear usually 12 to 24 hours after consumption of the contaminated item. They are nausea, vomiting, diarrhea, abdominal cramps, all more or less violent; headaches, chills, weakness, sometimes fever. Death is not uncommon if the afflicted are very young or aged or infirm.	Infection caused by consuming food containing salmonellae in large numbers. Many species and strains of *Salmonella* are capable of causing salmonellosis. *Source of organism:* the intestinal tract of man and animals and their waste products such as feces and urine, sewage, manure, and droppings; and everything	No toxin is released into food during multiplication; the bacteria set up infection in the gastrointestinal tract. Growth occurs in food at temperatures between 44 and 114°F. Excellent growth possible between 70 and 100°F. *Heat resistance* Heating to 165°F kills the majority of salmonellae.	Protein foods are excellent food for these bacteria. Meats, poultry, and cracked eggs are likely to be already contaminated when received and are doubly hazardous. Food items that have very frequently caused *Salmonella* food infections are turkey, stuffing and gravy; meat and poultry pies; cracked, undercooked eggs;	Food handler was ill with salmonellosis. Food handler did not wash, or superficially washed, hands after a visit to the toilet. Food handler did not wash hands after handling raw meat and poultry. Food handler did not thoroughly clean chopping blocks or other surfaces and equipment after	Persons suffering from salmonellosis or who are just recovering or who are carriers, must not handle food. All food handlers must thoroughly wash their hands after a visit to the toilet. Before starting work, the worker must wash his hands, and frequent hand washing must be practiced during preparation (after touching anything other than food, after touching food likely to be contaminated with salmonellae—meat, poultry, egg shells—and

Illness and Incidence	Brief Description of Illness	Cause and Main Source of Organisms Involved	Growth Requirements, Heat Resistance of Organism	Food Items Frequently Accused of Causing Illness	Circumstances Often Associated with Outbreaks	Principles of Control
		contaminated with human or animal excrements (which includes human hands, sewage-polluted water, and seafood); meat and poultry contaminated with animal excrement at slaughter; food preparation surfaces and equipment contaminated by contact with raw meat and poultry; food or surfaces contaminated by rodents and insects or leaking sewage (faulty plumbing).		chicken and turkey salads; meringue pies; and others too numerous to mention.	using them for raw meat and poultry. Rodents and flies had access to kitchen. Seafood from polluted water was used. Large stuffed turkey was prepared and under-cooked in center; contaminated giblets were added to gravy. Cracked eggs were used. Cooked food was exposed to warm temperatures. Leftovers were mishandled.	before touching other foods, especially cooked foods). Rodents and insects must be controlled. Food-preparation surfaces, equipment, and utensils must be kept in a sanitary condition. It is advised that separate cutting surfaces be used for raw and cooked items. Food should not be held at lukewarm temperatures. Keep food hot (140°F or above) or cold (45°F or below). Warm food should be cooled rapidly to safe temperatures.

Table VII. Perfringens Food Poisoning

Illness and Incidence of Illness	Brief Description of Illness	Cause and Main Source of Organisms Involved	Growth Requirements, Heat Resistance of Organism	Food Items Frequently Accused of Causing Illness	Circumstances Often Associated with Outbreaks	Principles of Control
Per-fringens Food Poisoning Incidence: less frequent than food-borne illnesses caused by staph and salmo-nellae	Symptoms usually appear 8 to 15 hours after consuming the contaminated item. They are similar to those caused by staph and salmonellae, but milder.	*Clostridium perfringens* *Source* of organism: Intestinal tract of humans and animals, soil, dust, equipment. Meats have good chance to become contaminated at time of slaughter. However, many	Growth occurs between 60 and 122°F; excellent growth between 109 and 116°F. *Heat resistance:* Some strains are very resistant to heat. We cannot rely on killing the spores by boiling, and must prevent organism from multiplying.	Meat and gravy are involved most frequently, especially beef and veal. Rolled roasts are apt to be contaminated on the inside, and are particularly hazardous when cooked to the rare stage.	Meat was cooked the previous day or several hours in advance, giving the bacteria a chance to multiply. Menu items were heavily contaminated with per-fringens bacteria adhering to hands and soiled equip-	Since the organism is everywhere, its presence in the kitchen—in dust, on equipment, on work tables, and on and in food—must be anticipated. Hands must be washed after raw meat has been handled. Work surfaces and food preparation equipment and utensils must be maintained in sanitary condition.

Table VII. (Continued)

Illness and Incidence	Brief Description of Illness	Cause and Main Source of Organisms Involved	Growth Requirements, Heat Resistance of Organism	Food Items Frequently Accused of Causing Illness	Circumstances Often Associated with Outbreaks	Principles of Control
		other foods have also been found to be contaminated with C. perfringens.			ment previously used for raw meat. Contaminated items were held neither hot enough nor cold enough.	C. perfringens is a spore former. Heating used in ordinary cooking cannot be relied on for killing the cells; therefore food must be kept out of the danger zone of bacterial growth as much as is possible. Keep food either hot (140°F or above) or cold (45°F or below). Warm food should be cooled rapidly to safe temperatures.

Index

Acceptance-type inspection service, 132
Acidity, effect on bacterial growth, 9-10; *see also*, pH
Agencies concerned with food protection, 120-121
Agitation in cooling fluid food, 166
Agricultural Marketing Service, 120, 132
Air, effect on bacterial growth, 9
Alkalinity, *see* pH
Amebae, 15
Amebic dysentery, 15, 204
Animals, poisonous, 48
   source of pathogens, 30-32, 40, 42, 44, 46, 203-207, 213-215
Antimony, 49
Asiatic cholera, 28, 205
Aspergillus, 12

Bacon, safety, 136
Bacteria, beneficial, 7
   benign, 7
   capable of causing food borne infections and intoxications, 33-47
   capable of causing illness, 7
   death, 7
   definition, 7, 16
   destruction, 10-12
   effect of temperature on, 10-12, 159-161
   growth conditions, 9-10
   growth curve, 8-9
   and man, 6-7
   multiplication in food, prevention, 159-186; *see also* Bacteria, growth conditions
   pathogenic, definition, 7
   psychrophilic, 10
   reproduction, 7-8; *see also* Bacteria

growth conditions
   resistance to freezing, 10
   resistance to heating, 10-11
   size and shape, 7
   spoilage, definition, 7
   spores, 7, 8
   thermophilic, 10
   toxin production, 9-10
Bacterial cells, vegetative, 7
Baked goods, creamfilled, recommendations for preparing, holding, 172
Baker's table, cleaning, 116-117
Bench can opener, cleaning, 91
Boards, *see* Chopping boards
Botulinum food poisoning, *see* Botulism
Botulism, 34, 36-37, 208-209
   foods frequently involved, 34, 36
   principles of control, 34, 36-37, 208-209
   symptoms, 34, 36, 208-209
Broiler, electric, overhead, cleaning, 102
Broom-sweeping, 70
Broth, *see* Soups, recommendations for preparing, holding
Brucellosis, 31, 206

Cadmium, 49
Cakes, crab and fish, recommendations for preparing, holding, 186
Canned food, purchase and storage, 140-141
   safety, 141
   spoilage, 25-26, 36-37
Can opener, bench, cleaning, 91
Carrier, definition, 16
   of pathogens, 199, 200, 202, 203, 204, 205, 212
Casseroles, bacteriologic safety, 157-159
   recommendations for preparing,

217

holding, 186
Cats, source of pathogens, 42
Ceilings, cleanability, 59-60
Checking and storing purchased food, 143-145
Checklist of items to be cleaned, 81-82
Cheese, bacteriologic safety, 125
Chemicals, poisoning by, 48-49
Chicken, see Poultry
Chilled food, see Chilling food
Chilled storage, of cooked items, 162-167
of deliveries, see specific items
see also specific items
Chilling food, 162-167
China, see Dishes
Cholera (Asiatic), 28, 205
Chopper, vegetable, cleaning, 84
Chopping boards, cleaning, 92
separate for raw and cooked foods, 156, 179
Chops, see Meat; Poultry
Clams, poisonous, 48; see also Fish and shellfish
Clean, cleaning, definitions, 16, 68, 78
Clean equipment and utensils, 78-119
facility (physical plant), 59-77
hands, 146, 150; see also Handwashing surfaces, 68
Cleaning material, utensils and equipment, storage area for, 67
Cleaning procedures, purpose, 67-68, 78-79
schedule, 68-69, 81-82
see also specific pieces of equipment
Clostridium botulinum, cause of botulism, 34, 36-37, 208-209
toxin, 34, 36, 209
Clostridium perfringens, 35, 44-46, 214-215
growth requirements, 46, 214
resistance to heat, 45-46, 214
sources and routes, 45
see also Perfringens food poisoning
Clothing, 149-150
Cockroaches, see Insects
Coffee urn, cleaning, 97-98
Cold, common, 28, 198
Cold cuts, safety, 136
Cold storage, see Chilled storage
Commodes, see Toilet bowls, cleaning
Communicable diseases, definition, 16
Contamination of food, see Food, con-taminated
Cooking, see Food, heating
Cooling, see Chilling food
Copper, 49
Cream, bacteriologic safety, 122, 123
fillings, recommendations for preparing, holding, 172
Creamed menu items, bacteriologic safety, 159
recommendations for preparing, holding, 171
Croquettes, recommendations for preparing, holding, 186
Crosscontamination, 15, 43-44, 156
Custards, baked, bacteriologic safety, 157
soft (stirred), recommendations for preparing, holding, 172
Cutter/mixer, vertical, cleaning, 85
Cutting (chopping) boards, cleaning, 92
separate, for raw and cooked foods, 156, 179

Dairy products, see Milk and other dairy products
Danger zone of bacterial growth, 10, 159-161
Definitions, see Terms, definition of
Defrosting procedures, 167-169
Deliveries, checking and storing, 143-145
Design for easy cleaning (equipment), 79
Desserts, chiffon-type, recommendations for preparing, holding, 175
egg-thickened, recommendations for preparing, holding, 172
frozen, bacteriologic safety, 126
made with uncooked egg, recommendation for preparing, holding, 175
whips, recommendations for preparing, holding, 175
Detergent, 78, 82
Diphtheria, 28, 202
Disease, transmission, 27-32, 198-207
Diseases, communicable, definition, 16
Dishes, carrying when serving, 149-151
washing, 95-96
Dish trucks, cleaning, 116
Dishwasher, flite type, cleaning, 111-112
sanitary aspects, 80-81
Dishwashing procedures, for dishes, glassware and flatware, 95-96

for pots, pans and small utensils, 93-94
Disinfectant, definition, 17
Displayed food, chilling, 167
Dogs, source of pathogens, 42
Dressing rooms, 62-63
Dry storage, 143-145
Dust-mopping, 72
Dysentery, amebic, 13, 15, 28, 204
    bacillary (shigellosis), 28, 203

Ears, infected, 38
Education in sanitation, 191-196
Egg, reconstituted from dried, 131
    salad, recommendations for preparing,
        holding, 184
    sandwiches, recommendations for pre-
        paring, holding, 185
Eggnog, recommendations for preparing,
    holding, 175
Eggs, cooked by various methods, safety,
    156-158
    dried, safety, 130-131
    frozen, safety, 130
    inspection, 127
    menu items containing, recommendations
        for preparing, holding, 172-175, 184-
        186
    pasteurized, 128
    processed, 128
    purchase and storage, 127-128, 129-131
    scrambled, 158
    shell, safety, 127-128, 129
    soft-cooked, 158
    storage, see Eggs, purchase and storage
    uncooked, menu items made with, 175
Eggs and egg-thickened products, heating,
    157, 158, 172
    recommendations for preparing, holding,
        172-175
Endameba histolytica, 13
Equipment, classification, 80-82
    checklist of items to be cleaned, 81-82
    cleanability, 59-60, 79
    cleaning procedures (to serve as a standard
        and training tool), 83-119
    in contact with food being processed, 80
    contaminatee, vehicle of pathogen trans-
        mission, 31
    design for easy cleaning, 79
    hot-holding, 162

installation, 79-80
    primary, used in cooking and holding
        food, 80
    transportation and mobile storage, 81-82
    used in cleaning other equipment, 80-81
Equipment and utensils, clean, 78-119
Eyes, infected, source of staphylococci, 38

Facility (physical plant), clean, 59-77
Federal inspection, see Inspection, govern-
    ment
Fillings, see Cream, fillings, recommenda-
    tions for preparing, holding
Fish and shellfish, fresh, safety, 139
    frozen, safety, 139
    items, recommendations for preparing,
        holding, 177, 184-186
    purchase and storage, 139-140
    smoked, safety, 139
Flatware, sanitary handling when serving
    food, 150
    washing, 95-96
Flies, see Insects
Floor drains, 60
Floors, cleanability, 59-60
    cleaning, 70-73
Food, bacterial multiplication in, 9-10, 159-
    169
    canned, see Canned food
    chemicals in, 48-49
    chilling, see Food, cooked, chilling
    contaminated, 152-154
    cooked, chilling, 162-167
        frozen, 167-169
        hot-holding, 162
    frozen, defrosting, 167-169; see also Foods,
        precooked, frozen
    handling and holding at hazardous tem-
        peratures, 159-162
    heating, thorough, 156-157
        mild, 157-159
        see also specific menu items
    infections, see Food, poisonings and food
        infections caused by bacteria
    intoxications, caused by agents other than
        microorganisms, 48-49
        caused by bacteria, 33-47
    leftover, see specific menu items
    moldy, 12
    perishability, 25-26

poisoning, 27
  caused by agents other than micro-
    organisms, 48-49
  poisonings and food infections caused by
    bacteria, 33-47
  preparation, sanitary (principles), 152-169
  protection, agencies, 120-121
    in food service establishment, 153-186
  purchase and storage, 120-145
  recontaminating, 15, 18, 43-44, 45
  spoilage, 25-26
  storage, see Food, purchase and storage
  toxic, definition, 19
  washing, 153
  wholesome, 152-154; see also specific
    menu items
Food and Drug Administration (FDA), 120
Foodborne illnesses, 27-53, 198-215
  incidence, 3, 52
  reporting and investigating, 50-53
Food for bacteria, 9-10
Food grinder, cleaning, 90
Food handler, attitude, 146-147
  cleanliness, 146, 149-151
  clothing, 150
  definition, 17
  hand habits, 146, 150-151
  health, 146-149
  personal hygiene, 146-150
  sanitation-conscious, 146-151
  source of pathogens, 28, 146
  work habits, 146-151, 193
Food mixer, cleaning, 88
Foods, pH of, 18
  potentially hazardous, 9-10, 18, 156
  precooked, frozen, 140-143
Food sanitation, education in, 191-195
  meaning of, 3-5
Food slicer, cleaning, 83
Food spoilage, 25-26
Food supply, agencies protecting, 120-121
  purchase and sanitary storage of, 120-145
Frankfurters, safety, 136
Freezing, effect on bacteria, 10
Frialator, electric, cleaning, 104
  gas, cleaning, 102-103
Fry pan, electric, cleaning, 104-105
Furuncles, source of staphylococci, 38

Garbage disposal, 63-64, 65

Gastroenteritis, definition, 17
Glassware, washing, 95-96
Gloves, 151, 154
Gravies, heating, 157-158
  recommendations for preparing, holding,
    178
Grinder, food, cleaning, 90

Habits, desirable, 193
Ham, bacteriologic safety, 135
  recommendations for preparing, holding,
    180
Hamburger, see Meat, ground
Hand habits, 146, 150; see also Habits,
  desirable
Hands, source of pathogens, 38-44, 46, 47,
  146
Handwashing, 150, 155-156
  facilities, 61-62
Heating food to kill dangerous contaminants,
  general recommendations, 156-159;
  see also specific menu items
Hepatitis, infectious, 28, 205
Hollandaise, recommendations for preparing,
  holding, 174
Hood and hood filter, cleaning, 76
Hot-holding equipment, 162
Hot-holding of prepared menu items, 162
Hygiene, personal, definition, 17
  rules for food handlers, 147-149

Ice cream and similar frozen desserts, bac-
  teriologic safety, 126
Ice cream cabinet, cleaning, 112-113
Illnesses, foodborne, see Foodborne illnesses
Infections, foodborne, see Food, poisonings
  and Food infections caused by bacteria
Influenza, 28, 202
Insects, control, 30-31, 64-67
  vehicles of pathogen transmission, 30-31
Inspection, government, 120-121
Installation for easy cleaning (equipment),
  79
Intestinal diseases, transmission, 28-29, 203-
  205
Intestinal tract, source of pathogenic bacteria,
  see Salmonella Food infection; Per-
  fringens food poisoning; Streptococcus
  food infection
Intoxications, foodborne, see

Food, intoxications
Investigation of food poisoning outbreaks,
   50-53

J.I.T., motto, 195
   technique, 194
Job breakdown, 194

Kettle, cooling, 166
   steamjacketed, cleaning, 99-100
Kitchen temperatures, 161-162

Lag phase of bacterial growth, 8
   definition, 18
Lead, 49
Leftovers, *see* specific menu items
Lighting, 61
Lights, cleaning, 77
Livestock, source of pathogens, 31, 41-42,
   44, 46, 206-207
Locker rooms, *see* Dressing rooms
Logarithmic (or log) phase of bacterial
   growth, definition, 18

Man, source of pathogens, 6-7, 38-47
Mayonnaise, recommendations for preparing,
   holding, 175
   use in salads, sandwiches, 184, 185
Meat, contamination, 132-133
   cooked by various methods, safety, 156-
      158
   fresh, safety, 134-135
   frozen, safety, 137
   ground, heating, 158
      items, recommendations for preparing,
         holding, 186
      safety, 134
   inspection, 128, 132-133
   items, recommendations for preparing,
      holding, 179-180, 184-186
   pies, heating, 159
      recommendations for preparing, holding,
         186
   purchase and storage, 128, 132-140
   roasts, heating, 157-158
      recommendations for preparing, holding,
         179
      safety, 134, 137
   see also, Ham; Pork
   safety, 134-137

salads, *see* Salads, recommendations for
   preparing, holding
sandwiches, *see* Sandwiches, recommendations for preparing, holding
saw (power), cleaning, 89-90
source of pathogens, 132-133
storage, *see* Purchase and sanitary storage
   of food supply
Meats, heating, 156-158
   variety, safety, 135
Menu items, made with comminuted meat,
      poultry, egg, fish, shellfish, recom-
      mendations for preparing, holding,
      186
   creamed, 159, 171
   hazardous, safety, 170-186
   heated, mildly, 157-159
      thoroughly, 156-157
   much-handled, 158-159, 186
   see also Food; Foods
Meringued pies, recommendations for preparing, holding, 173
Metals, poisoning by, 49
Mice, *see* Rodents
Microorganisms, basic facts, 6-15
   prevention of multiplication in food, 159-
      186
   see also Bacteria; Molds; Protozoa; Tri-
      chinae; Viruses; Yeasts
Milk, condensed, safety, 124
   dried, reconstituted, safety, 125-126
      safety, 124-125
   evaporated, safety, 123
   fermented, safety, 122
   fluid, safety, 122
   pasteurized, 121, 125
Milk and other dairy products, purchase
      and storage, 121-127
   safety, 122-125
Mirrors, cleaning, 77
Mixer, food, cleaning, 88; *see also* Cutter/
      mixer, vertical, cleaning
Moisture for bacterial growth, 10
Molds, 12
Moldy food, *see* Food, moldy
Mopping, *see* Dust-mopping
Mouth, source of staphylococci, 38
Multiplication, bacterial, at kitchen tempera-
      tures, 161-162
   when chilling food, 162-167

when displaying food, 167
when handling frozen food, 167-169
when holding prepared food hot, 162
see also, Bacteria, growth conditions;
   Bacteria, growth curve
Mushroom poisoning, 48
Mussels, poisonous, 48; see also Fish and
   shellfish

Nails, clean, 149
National Sanitation Foundation, 4, 79
Nose, source of staphylococci, 38

Oven, electric stack, cleaning, 109
   gas stack, cleaning, 109
   range, cleaning, 108
Oysters, see Fish and shellfish

Pans, see Pots, pans and small utensils,
   cleaning
Parasites, definition, 18
Pasteurization, definition, 18
   of milk, 121-122
Pathogen, definition, 18
Patties (meat, poultry, seafood) recommendations for preparation, holding,
   186
Performance evaluation, standard, 82
Perfringens food poisoning, 35, 44-46, 214-
   215
   foods frequently involved, 35, 44
   principles of control, 35, 46, 214-215
   symptoms, 35, 44, 214
Perishable foods, 25-26
Pets, see Cats, source of pathogens, Dogs,
   source of pathogens
pH, definition, 18
   effect on bacterial growth, 9-10
   of various foods, 18
Physical plant, see Facility (physical plant),
   clean
Pies, see Meat, pies; Meringued pies, recom-
   mendations for preparing, holding;
   Poultry, pies
Pimples, source of staphylococci, 38
Plants, poisonous, 48
Platform scales, cleaning, 91
Plumbing, 60
Pneumonia, 28, 200
Pork, bacteriologic safety, 134-137

recommendations for preparing, holding,
   180
trichinae in, 14-15
see also Trichinae; Trichinosis
Portion-control scales, cleaning, 92
Pot-and-pan machine, cleaning, 110-111
Potato peeler, cleaning, 98-99
Potato poisoning, 48
Potato salad, see Salads, recommendations
   for preparing, holding
Potentially hazardous foods, see Foods,
   potentially hazardous
Pots, pans and small utensils, cleaning, 93-94
Poultry, contamination, 132-133
   cooked by various methods, safety, 156-
   158
   deboning, recommendations, 182-183
   fresh, safety, 138
   frozen, safety, 138
   heating, 156-158
   inspection, 128, 132-133
   items, recommendations for preparing,
   holding, 181-186
   pies, heating, 159
   recommendations for preparation,
   holding, 186
   purchase and storage, 128, 132-133, 138
   safety, 138
   salads, see Salads, recommendations for
   preparing, holding
   sandwiches, see Sandwiches, recommendations for preparing, holding
   source of pathogens, 132-133
   storage, see Purchase and sanitary storage
   of Food supply
Power meat saw, cleaning, 89-90
Practice, sanitary, 57-190
Preparing and holding food, sanitary procedures, 152-169
Procedures, sanitary, see Practice, sanitary
Protein foods, 38
Protozoa, 13, 15
Psychrophilic bacteria, 10
Ptomaine food poisoning, definition, 18
Puddings, recommendations for preparing,
   holding, 172
Purchase and sanitary storage of food supply,
   120-145
   canned foods, 140-141
   eggs, 127-128, 129-131

fish and shellfish, 139, 140
meat and poultry, 128, 132-138, 140
milk and other dairy products, 121-127
poultry, *see* Purchase and sanitary storage
of food supply, meat and poultry
precooked frozen foods, 141-142

Range ovens, cleaning, 108
Ranges, cleaning, 106-107
Rats, *see* Rodents
Recontaminating, *see* Food, recontaminating
Refrigerating, *see* Chilling food
Refrigerator, cleaning, 114
storage, 144-145
see also specific items
Reporting of food poisoning outbreaks, 50-53
Respiratory diseases, transmission, 28-29,
198-202
Respiratory tract, source of foodpoisoning
bacteria, *see Staphylococcus* food
poisoning
Roasts, bacteriologic safety, 157-158
recommendations for preparing, holding,
179-180
Rodents, control, 30-31, 64-67
source of pathogens, 30-31
Rules to safeguard wholesomeness of prepared menu items, 152-154

Safe temperatures for holding food,
definition, 19
Salad dressing, *see* Mayonnaise
Salads, recommendations for preparing, holding, 184
Salamander, *see* Broiler, electric, overhead,
cleaning
Salmonella, in animals, 42
cause of Salmonellosis, 35, 40-44, 212-213
in food supply, 42-43
growth requirements, 43, 212
in man, 40-42
resistance to heat, 43, 212
in sewage, 42
sources and routes, 40-42
Salmonella food infection, 35, 40-44, 212-213
carrier state, 40
foods frequently involved, 35, 43-44,

212-213
principles of control, 35, 43-44, 212-213
symptoms, 35, 40, 212
Salmonellosis, *see Salmonella* food infection
Sandwiches, recommendations for preparing,
holding, 185
Sanitary practice, 57-190
Sanitary preparation of food, general principles, 152-169
Sanitation, *see* Food sanitation
Sanitizing, definition, 19, 78-79
Scales, platform, cleaning, 91
portion control, cleaning, 92
table, cleaning, 92
Scarlet fever, 28, 199
Scrubbing, 73
Seafood, *see* Fish and shellfish; Salads, recommendations for preparing, holding;
Sandwiches, recommendations for
preparing, holding
Septic sore throat, 28, 199
Serving food in a sanitary manner, 148-151
Sewage, as contaminant of food, water, 30,
40, 44
disposal, 60
Shellfish certification, 140
contaminated by sewage, 30
poisonous, 48
purchase and storage, 139-140
recommendations for preparing, holding,
177
salads, *see* Salads, recommendations for
preparing, holding
see also Fish and shellfish
Shelving, metal, cleaning, 119
poisonous, 49
Shigellosis, *see* Dysentery, bacillary
Silverware, *see* Flatware
Sinks, pot-and-pan, sanitary aspects, 80-81
Sinuses, infected, source of pathogens, 28,
38
Slicer, food, cleaning, 83
Smoking, 150, 151
Soil, source of pathogens, 30, 36, 44
Sores, infected, source of pathogens, 38
Sore throat, septic, 199
Souffles, 157
Soups, recommendations for preparing, holding, 176
Sources of pathogens causing foodborne ill-

nesses, *see* specific illnesses
Spoilage, *see* Food, spoilage
Spores, bacterial, 7
  mold, 12
Stack ovens, cleaning, 109
Staphylococcus aureus, cause of staph food
    poisoning, 34, 37-39, 210-211
  growth requirements, 39, 210
  resistance to heat, 39, 210
  sources and routes, 38-39
  toxin, 37, 39, 210
Staphylococcus food poisoning, 34, 37-39,
    210-211
  foods frequently involved, 34, 210-211
  principles of control, 34, 39, 210-211
  symptoms, 34, 210
Steak machine, cleaning, 88
Steaks, *see* Meat; Poultry
Steamer, hi-pressure, cleaning, 100-101
  stack, cleaning, 100
Steamjacketed kettle, *see* Kettle, steam-
    jacketed, cleaning
Steam table, cleaning, 115
Storage, of cleaning materials, utensils,
    equipment, 67
  dry, 143
  of food supply, 120-145
    canned food, 140-141
    eggs, 127-128, 129-131
    fish and shellfish, 139, 140
    meat and poultry, 128, 132-138, 140
    milk and other dairy products, 121-127
    poultry, *see* Meat; Poultry
    precooked frozen foods, 141-142
  of prepared food, 159-161, 162-167, 170-
    186
Streptococcus food infection, 46-47
Sweeping, *see* Broom-sweeping

Tables, baker's, cleaning, 116-117
  kitchen, cleaning, 118
Table scales, cleaning, 92
Tableware, *see* Dishes; Flatware; Glassware,
    washing
Tasting food, 151
Temperature, effect on bacteria, 10-12, 159-
    161
  of water, for cleaning, 78
  for sanitizing, 78-79
Temperature control, of bacteria when chil-

ling cooked food, 162-167
  when handling frozen food, 167-169
  when handling and holding food in kitchen,
    161-162
  when heating food, 156-159
  when holding cooked food hot, 162
Temperatures, hazardous, 10, 159-161
  for pasteurization, 121
  for storage, *see* Storage
Terms, definition of, 16-20
Thawing, *see* Defrosting procedures
Thermophilic, definition, 10, 19
Thermoduric, definition, 19
Throat, septic sore, 28, 199
  source of staphylococci, 38
Time-temperature control of bacteria, defi-
    nition, 19
Toaster, automatic, cleaning, 96-97
  rotary, cleaning, 96
Toilet bowls, cleaning, 76-77
Toilet facilities, 62-63
Tonsilitis, 28, 200
Toxins, definition, 19
  resistance to heating, *see Clostridium
    botulinum; Staphylococcus aureus*
Trainer, qualifications, 193-194
Training food service personnel in sanita-
    tion, 191-196
  basic steps in, 194-195
  plan and schedule, 194-195
  tool, 81-82
Transmission of disease, 27-32, 198-207
Trench mouth, 28, 201
Trichinae, 14-15, 157, 180
Trichinosis, 31, 207
Tuberculosis, 28, 201
Tularemia, 31, 206
Turkey, 157, 158; *see also* Poultry
Typhoid fever, 28, 203

Urinals, cleaning, 76-77
U. S. Department of Agriculture (USDA),
    120-121, 127, 132-133
U. S. Department of Health, Education
    and Welfare (HEW), 120-121
U. S. Food and Drug Administration (FDA),
    120-121
U. S. Public Health Service (PHS), 120-121
Utensils, contaminated, vehicles of pathogen
    transmission, 31

small, cleaning, 93-94
use of, in serving food, 151

Vegetable chopper, cleaning, 84
Vegetative cells, 77
Vehicle of transmission, definition, 19
Ventilation, 61
Vermin, *see* Insects; Rodents
Viruses, 13
Visual aids for training personnel, 196

Wallpaper, cleaning, 75
Walls, care of, 73-75
  cleanability, 59-60
Warmth for bacterial growth, 10
Washbowls, cleaning, 76-77

Waste disposal, *see* Garbage disposal
Water, as cleaning agent, 78-79
  hot, as sanitizing agent, 11-12, 78-79
  polluted, source of pathogens, 30
Wet-mopping, 72-73
White sauce, *see* Creamed menu items,
    bacteriologic safety
Wholesomeness of prepared food, 152-154
Windows, cleaning, 77
Woodwork, cleaning, 74, 75
Wounds, infected, source of staphylococci,
    38

Yeasts, 13

Zinc, 49